Beyond the Himalayas : a story of travel and adventure in the wilds of Thibet

John Geddie

BEYOND THE HIMALAYAS.

A STORY OF TRAVEL AND ADVENTURE IN
THE WILDS OF THIBET.

BY

JOHN GEDDIE,

AUTHOR OF "THE LAKE REGIONS OF CENTRAL AFRICA."
ETC. ETC.

WITH ILLUSTRATIONS.

London:
T. NELSON AND SONS, PATERNOSTER ROW.
EDINBURGH; AND NEW YORK.
1884.

Preface.

THE problem of opening up an overland route from the Ganges to the Yang-tze——a subject which has long piqued and baffled the curiosity of their seniors——ought to have some attraction for the imagination of young people, if, as formerly, they take delight in wandering among strange and wild scenes, and in encountering manifold obstacles and dangers. Many have sought of late years to climb over the division-wall between the two crowded Eastern worlds of India and China,——the trader, to find a new market for his wares; the explorer, in search of a whole nest of "Chinese puzzles" regarding the courses of giant rivers and mountain chains; and the missionary, in pursuit of his self-denying labours. Only at one point, however, and by a roundabout way, has the journey been accomplished. This is not wonderful, when we reflect that the traveller in these countries must run the gauntlet of savage mountain tribes, jealous

Chinese officials, and fanatical Thibetan lamas, in addition
to surmounting the extraordinary natural difficulties of
crossing the frayed-out ends of the Himalayas that
interpose between the Assam frontier and China proper.
The surface of this unexplored region is wrinkled up
into deep folds, like the hide of a rhinoceros; and down
these furrows five rivers of the first rank are known
to flow, though their channels have never been traced
throughout.   Their sources are in the most remote
nooks of the table-land of Thibet, and their waters
find an outlet at points so far apart as Calcutta and
Shanghai.   But here for a space their main courses are
drawn together within a narrow compass, resembling, to
use the expression of Colonel Yule, the learned editor
of "Marco Polo," "the fascis of thunderbolts in the
clutch of Jove, or the parallel lines of railway at Clap-
ham Junction."   It is over this, the most difficult bit of
"cross country" perhaps in the world, that Bob Brown
seeks to lead the reader; and as there is no authentic
record of the same line of country having been traversed,
it is impossible to say how nearly his narrative will be
found to agree with facts.   At the same time the scenery
and manners described resemble what might be expected
from the relations of the distinguished French and
English explorers—Huc, Carné, Cooper, Margary, Baber,
Gill, and others—who have penetrated into South-
Western China and Thibet.

Contents.

BEYOND THE HIMALAYAS.

CHAPTER I.

"MYSTERIES."

" WONDER what lies beyond?"

We were sitting, a group of four Europeans, in the veranda of a bunga-low into which an Indian sunset was shining. The scene was intensely tropical and Eastern. Climbing plants twined up the trellis-work of the veranda, festooning the pillars with masses of broad green leaves, starred with brilliant purple and scarlet flowers. In the garden beyond were clumps of foliage and blossom of types which "at home" you are accustomed to see only in a conservatory. But here, instead of the dwarfed and drooping exotics that pine and grow pale in exile, the plants had a free, vigorous growth that showed that they were breathing native air. It

was like the difference, in fact, between a collection
of wild animals cooped up in a menagerie and the same
creatures roaming free in their forest haunts. Fruits,
too, some of them familiar, but many of them strange
and rare, shone out temptingly from amid the dusk of the
leaves like great golden orbs, or in clusters. The huge,
clumsy form of an elephant could be descried moving
up one of the avenues towards the house, his pendulous
trunk swinging to and fro in unison with his deliberate
step, and only occasionally vouchsafing a discontented
grunt in reply to the appeals of the mahout to increase
his speed. A native gardener, dressed, like the elephant
driver, in white calico, which made a striking contrast
with his dusky face, was approaching in an equally
leisurely manner, bearing on his shoulders the hoes and
other tools with which he had been trimming the walks.
Other black attendants were preparing the hookahs for
the last evening smoke, and removing the cups from
which we had been drinking a fragrant draught of tea;
while in the large chamber behind, on the other side of
the green jalousies, the lamps were being lighted.

All this spoke unmistakably of Hindostan.

But looking away from the house, over the wide
prospect that the veranda commanded, there were
features in the landscape that would have struck an
Anglo-Indian as not familiar in Indian scenery. A long
hill-slope stretched down in front of us, covered with

dark masses of virgin forest, between which were wide
clearings, planted with short, trimly-kept shrubs, that a
practised eye might have recognized to be young tea-
trees. At a distance of a mile and a half, or rather
more, a great river flowed through the valley in many
channels, separated from each other by islands densely
covered with sal-trees, bamboos, and reeds, and broad
belts of the same vegetation bounded the two shores.
Our bungalow looked partly across and partly up the
stream, on the other side of which wood-covered hills
rose peak behind peak, with deep ravines seaming their
sides, and dark valleys winding between their folds,
until their colours and shapes seemed to melt into those
of the array of clouds attending upon the sun, who was
about to set behind them. How shall I describe the
splendours of that tropical evening—the gorgeous richness and the harmony of the piled-up masses of vapour,
the soft glow of the unfathomable depths of rosy, pearly,
and cream-coloured sky that lay between, and the
flood of level light that poured across the mountains
from the descending sun ? It is indescribable ; one
must see such a picture with his own eyes in order
to have a conception of its beauty. The shadows were
already falling on the river: some figures that we
had been watching as they moved through the reeds
might be a group of tame buffaloes that had not
yet been driven home ; or a troop of wild cattle

taking possession of one of their island strongholds; or it might even be native boatmen punting their way up one of the narrow creeks, so dim had their outlines become.

The light, however, struck on another great range of mountains on the hither side of the stream, whose purple sides rose like a mysterious and impassable wall on our extreme right. It was in the direction of this range that the speaker's eyes were turned as he pronounced the words that stand at the opening of the chapter. I have to introduce him first, as by far the most important personage in this narrative. You had only to glance at Dr. Roland to see that he was no ordinary man either in physique or intellect. At least that is what I felt when I first set eyes on him; and my " chum," Tom Wilson, felt exactly the same. His face and neck had been burned a ruddy brown by exposure to many a blazing sun, and deep study had ploughed one or two wrinkles in his broad brow, though he was still a man under middle age. There was no trace of the fatigue and hardships he had endured in travelling all over the globe, in his tall, powerful figure. His eye had none of the supercilious or abstracted expression that repels one in some men of learning; it was bright and kindly, and alert like his step. I shall not describe his features in detail, and need only say that his face inspired you from the first with confidence and respect, and that you afterwards learned to love it. I know that when we heard—my friend Tom and I—that so great a man was coming to visit us, we felt a great awe of him. We never entirely lost that awe, but it soon became merged in the strong personal attachment which we learned to entertain for him.

He had come to spend a few weeks with his old friend Mr. Marshall, who had settled in the most remote district of Upper Assam, and with whom Tom Wilson and your humble servant—I forgot to introduce myself as Robert, or, as my familiar acquaintances choose to call me, Bob Brown—had been living for nearly a year, learning the business of tea-planting. The doctor brought, along with his inseparable negro servant Hannibal, whom he had rescued from a dismal swamp in Louisiana where the poor hunted fellow had found shelter from a brutal slave-master, a wonderful collection of explorers' apparatus—quadrants, chronometers, thermometers, aneroids, botanical cases, collecting boxes, and I know not what else; besides rifles and other instruments of the chase,— for his love of sport was only second to his love of science. A wing of the bungalow was set apart for his use, and over it Hannibal lay in watch like a dragon; but we were often of an evening privileged to enter the doctor's sanctum, and looked on with breathless interest while he made experiments or classified the plants and animals he had secured during his day's tramp, good-naturedly making for our benefit a running commentary on the habits and peculiarities of the beetles, spiders, and ants that he tenderly spitted on pins, and of the mosses, lichens, orchids, and ferns that he carefully spread out and pressed to death in the interests of science. Sometimes, too, we had had the treat of accompanying him on his sporting excursions to the hills or in the jungles along the river side, and had under his eye bowled over many a head of forest game, such as wild pig and deer, though our teacher in the art had hitherto taken the post of danger, and had reserved to his own gun the tigers, buffaloes, rhinoceroses, elephants, and bears that had come in our way.

It was not strange that in the circumstances we had come to regard Dr. Roland with enthusiastic admiration; that there was nothing that we would not have done to show our devotion to him, and that, in our view, there was scarcely anything that he did not know as familiarly as the alphabet. It was therefore with some surprise as well as curiosity that we watched him gazing away towards those eastern hills, with a baffled and eager air, and heard him express his "wonder" as to what was on the other side.

"Can you not tell us, then, sir," said Tom, who was the first to break the silence, "what is beyond that big wall?"

"Mystery," said the doctor, dropping his voice to a stage whisper, but looking all the while more than half serious. "Do you know, young fellows," he continued, "that fate has placed you in the one nook of the inhabitable earth around which a little romance still lingers? And yet you can find nothing more heroic to do than killing chickens." (This was a bantering reference to an exploit of mine on the previous day, when I had shot a fowl, that had strayed away to the edge of the plantation, in mistake for a pheasant.) "There is mystery brooding all about you, except along the valley there by which you came up hither from Calcutta. Those heights across the river, behind which the sun is just about to hide himself, are, as you know, the foothills of the great Himalaya. Can any of you tell me the secrets of their recesses? No; neither then can I. That huge mountain range stretches from here to Afghanistan; nay, as I could show you, to the Caucasus and the Crimea. There is nothing like it in the world for height and grandeur. Its base rises directly from the hot steaming plains of India, and ascends tier above tier like a vast staircase of mountains till it carries you to glittering heights, thousands of feet above the line of perpetual snow, that will never be trodden by man. If you climb up by one of the passes, until your head swims and you catch your breath in short gasps by reason of the rarity of the air, you will find that there is, comparatively speaking, no slope to descend."

" Then, has the Himalaya only one side ?" I asked.

" Yes, Bob; and on the top is Thibet and the Roof of the World."

" And what happens to you after you get on the roof ?"

" You remember what happened to the Duke of York and his ten thousand men ?" said Mr. Marshall, smiling. " He marched them up a hill, and marched them down again. I wouldn't advise you, Master Bob, to attempt that climb. The Thibetans might take a fancy not to let you away at all, but nail you up on the frontier as a warning to other trespassers, as a gamekeeper does a weasel."

" Why should they make such a fuss about their stupid country ?" said Tom in a tone of disgust. " I never heard that there was anything very pretty to be seen there."

" It is the Holy Land of one of the great religions of the world, my boy," said the doctor. " It is made sacred by being the residence of the Grand Lama, the living Buddha, and must be kept pure from the profane feet of unbelievers, who might besides take a fancy to occupy the country. They have guarded their frontiers well. I believe that you could count on the fingers of one hand all the Europeans who have penetrated to the heart of Thibet. I think it is very foolish policy, however. It is a cold, wild, and barren region. If the lamas opened their doors to strangers, they would soon satisfy their curiosity and go away. But as long as they keep the world waiting outside, the world will want to get in. But leaving that matter aside, look at that great river there, the Bramaputra, coming full-grown from the hills, with no fountain-head that any one knows of. Isn't that a mystery? There is no stream of its size about which there is so much conjecture."

"I thought the maps made it out to be the Sanpoo," said Tom Wilson meekly.

"You mustn't pin your faith to all you find in maps," the doctor replied. "Some of the wildest and most fanciful romances extant are to be found in these lines of mountain ranges, rivers, and deserts which the geographers trace for you. In this case they have heard of a stream that flows through the highlands of Thibet, and then they perceive a flood of waters issuing from the hills to meet the Ganges. The river of the cold, bare highlands above is no more like the tropical stream below there than the hard-featured Thibetan is like the mild Hindu ; and they run in opposite directions. But the people that make the maps don't know whither the one goes, nor from whence the other comes——"

"And so," interrupted Mr. Marshall, "they join the

head of the first to the tail of the second, and construct
a monster like the mermaid that the Yankee showman
made out of a monkey and a fish. But come now,
doctor, what better splice could you make yourself than
these yarning map-makers ?"

"I could not do a bit better," said our sage, shaking
his head. "I daresay they are right. But just think
what might happen in that mysterious gap. Why, the
Sanpoo must fall over a score of precipices, cut all sorts
of strange capers, and be terribly shaken ,and jumbled
before it becomes the Bramaputra. What is to hinder
it from diving wholly underground, letting this river
flow over the top of it, then popping up on the other
side and going off to join the Irrawady ?

"Come, come, my friend," said Mr. Marshall, laughing;
"this beats the maps hollow as a fiction."

"It is not so utterly impossible as you fancy," responded Dr. Roland gravely. "All sorts of queer things
happen up there with the rivers. They have a trick of
disappearing in the earth, and coming to the surface
again miles and miles away, after traversing 'caverns
measureless to man,' like Alph, the Sacred River that
ran by the palace of the great Kublai Khan. By the
way, youngsters," he went on, suddenly turning to us,
"you have read Marco Polo's travels of course ?"

"No," I answered shamefacedly.

Tom plucked up a little courage on the strength of

his having once "ground up" the history of the medi-
eval traveller as an examination subject, and, of course,
had long ago forgotten it; so he was beginning,—
"Wasn't that the old Venetian bloke that—"

"Please don't call Marco Polo a 'bloke,'" broke in the
doctor sternly; "indeed, I am not sure that it is proper
to describe any one by that title. But the great ones
of the earth at least must be spoken of with respect;
and you would never talk of Christopher Columbus, or
Vasco da Gama, or David Livingstone, as a 'bloke.'
Brave old Marco is one of the same glorious band; and
I cannot fancy anything more entrancing to young
fellows like you, or to your elders either, than the story
of his marvellous journey across Asia, if only you put
your head into what you read, as, of course, every one
should, and try to see with your 'mind's eye' what he
describes in his quaint language. What wild, unfre-
quented regions he carries you into! What giddy
heights you scale, and what abysses you cross, from the
time that you land with the needy soldier of fortune on
the shores of Asia Minor until you see him return, loaded
with Tartar wealth and honours, to his native city. You
are brought by the cities of Samarcand and Balkh, over
the Pamir steppe, and across deserts of sand and stones
and salt by a route that no Western traveller has since
been able to follow; and you hear strange tidings by the
way of the Old Man of the Mountain, of Prester John, of

Gog and Magog, of wild camels and hairy oxen, of mines
of sapphire, jasper, and chalcedony, and of the mysterious
voices that haunt the Wilderness of Lob. Then when you
reach the Court of the Grand Khan, what barbaric riches
and splendour you witness within and without the royal
palace, whose walls are thirty-two miles in circuit,—the
great hall where the fierce Tartar warriors, who had
perhaps fought their way across the world from Japan
to Germany, drank wine out of flagons of gold; the
hunting parties that set out in chase of the lion and
smaller game, with falcons and leashes of leopards and
lynxes; and the splendid stud of milk-white horses
from which the chargers of the princes were chosen.
After that you pass on through exceeding rich, powerful,
and magnificent cities, and across broad and noble
rivers—"

"Stop, stop!" cried Mr. Marshall. "See how you are
making the eyes of these lads sparkle with your stories
of worthy Signor Polo's travels! They will be packing
their bundles and setting out in quest of his river with
sands of gold dust, and perhaps will fall into the jaws
of that wonderful serpent of his with claws like a tiger
and glaring eyes 'bigger than a fourpenny loaf.' Tell
us rather about your plan for your own trip up the
mountains next week."

"I was just coming to that," said the doctor. "Marco's
River of Gold Sands is on the other side of these moun-

tains. If we could 'interview' him, I daresay he could tell us more of the country beyond than any one knows to-day, for we have learned very little in the six hundred years since he wandered through China. I intend, if I have time, to go as far up through the hills as possible, with the hope of seeing a little into the heart of the mystery."

Tom and I exchanged eager glances. We had been promised two or three weeks' holidays, and it was our cherished hope that we would be allowed to spend them with Dr. Roland. You may be sure that when we heard what his route was to be we became more than ever ardent in our wish to accompany him.

"Where does the road lie over these hills?" began Tom.

"That is exactly the question," said the doctor, knitting his brows musingly. "Nobody can say that there is a road at all. Here we are within a comparatively few miles of the confines of China, and we might, for all we see or hear of it, be as many thousand leagues away. There must be somewhere up there an 'iron wall' of division between India and China; and it has kept apart five or six hundred millions of people—half the inhabitants of the earth—down to this day. When they have met either for trade or war, they have had to make a vast circuit by Cabul and Kashgar, or some other roundabout road."

" Is it impassable, then, sir ? "

" I don't much believe either in 'impassable' or 'impossible.'   I daresay there is a way of clambering over the obstacle if one could only hit it.   I fancy that stork there going home to roost knows the clue; or if he is not high-flier enough, some of the hill vultures could tell you."

" What do you think one would find if he got over, sir ?" I asked.

" Well, Bob, that lucky man would probably find a deep valley, ending in a chasm with precipitous walls and a river at the bottom—what they call in America a cañon; and if he managed to scramble down without breaking his neck, and embarked on the stream, he would be shot down cataracts and shot at by wild tribes for many weeks, and at length find himself sailing down the Irrawady, past the Peacock Palace of Mandalay, the thousand temples of Pagham, and the Golden Pagoda of Rangoon, to the sea."

" That would be a lucky man indeed," said Mr. Marshall, laughing.

" But if he despised following the river, and scaled the range of mountains beyond," continued the doctor, " he would come upon just such another ravine and stream, and this would carry him a thousand miles and more through a wild, untraversed back-country, amid half-barbarous Shans and wholly savage Karens,—perhaps past the mines of rubies and sapphires of the king of Ava,—until he would find himself at the mouth of the Salwen, in the British harbour of Moulmein, in the Bay of Bengal."

"And suppose he despised the Salwen too, and skipped over it—which is the only way I see of crossing it?" asked the master of the house.

"Then at a short distance, measured by space, but terribly long in time, for it would carry him high up among the clouds, he would find a third and still greater river—the Mekong. And if he built for himself a bark canoe, and his luck still clung to him, he would pass amid scenes of incredible grandeur and terror, through the very heart of Indo-China, emerging at last among the French settlers in Saigon. If the Mekong itself were not good enough for the attention of this haughty explorer, he would only have to go a stage or two further, and after another sojourn in the mountains of Thibet, he might get afloat on the River of Golden Sand,—the head-waters of the mighty Yang-tze-Kiang itself,—and descend, past junks and joss-houses, pagodas and porcelain towers, exchanging nods with mandarins and bonzes, to the Pacific Ocean. So, instead of one 'iron wall,' there are four lines of ramparts at least, with a deep trench between each, separating us from the Flowery Land."

"May Tom and I go with you to the hills, sir?" said

I, after a pause, looking appealingly from the doctor to
Mr. Marshall, Tom meanwhile seconding the request with
his eyes.

It was now the turn of the elders to exchange
glances.

"You would be of great use to me, boys, I admit,"
said the doctor gravely; "but the journey will be a
rough one and not without some danger. There have
been stories, you know, of the hill tribes being restless. You would be away three weeks at least, and
I do not know that Mr. Marshall can spare you for
so long."

"Let us go inside and talk the matter over," said Mr.
Marshall. "It is already almost dark, and the dews are
beginning to fall."

When we were all seated round the table in the
bungalow, it was settled, after serious consideration, that
Tom and I should accompany Dr. Roland; and we then
proceeded—or rather our elders proceeded, while we
listened eagerly—to discuss the arrangements for the
journey. It was long ere excitement would allow me to
fall asleep that night; and when at length I dozed off, I
dreamed that I was Marco Polo, and that, mounted on a
shaggy yak, I was fleeing from a hideous dragon with
saucer eyes that chased me up steep hills and across
yawning gulfs, at the bottom of which I could hear
water gurgling and roaring through caverns while the

crashes of the stones as they bumped from rock to rock into the abyss sounded loudly in my ears. Awakening, I found that my neighbour Tom, also suffering from nightmare, was snorting violently in his sleep and wildly beating the wall with his fists.

CHAPTER II.

THE JOURNEY INTO THE HILLS.

BRIGHT and early one morning, a week after the conversation recorded in last chapter, we set out on our journey to the mountains. So early was it that some of the stars had not faded from the sky, and the fog had not yet cleared away from the banks of the Bramaputra when we turned our backs upon it and our faces towards the sunrise, beginning to glimmer over these hills which we had come to associate with all that is mystic and marvellous. Our heavier luggage was packed upon the backs of two elephants. One carried our tent, hammocks, and the warm clothing which we expected to require on the cold mountain-tops to which we were bound. Hannibal— who would, I believe, have undertaken to drive a giraffe or a hippopotamus in the service of his master—was in charge of the other huge beast (Ghenghiz by name), and from his elevated seat glanced with an air of calm pride at the cooking apparatus, the doctor's scientific instruments, and the packages containing preserved meat, cartridges, and spare rifles that were neatly arranged behind him. Hannibal—or Han, as we were accustomed to call him—would have made a capital " study in black and white" for an artist. It is impossible to imagine anything blacker than his skin or whiter than his newly-washed cotton uniform, or than the whites of his eyes and his rows of shining teeth, as he grinned delightedly in acknowledgment of a word of praise which the doctor gave him for his arrangements. The only neutral tint about him was his hair (his wool rather), which was becoming grizzled with age ; but though past his youth, Han was still possessed of enormous strength. He was a faithful, honest fellow, in whom we were not long in discovering a thousand good qualities that we had not expected. He was kind enough to take a patronizing interest in us youngsters, though we suspected all the time that he would have little hesitation in cooking either of us for his master's breakfast, if Dr. Roland expressed the slightest wish in that direction. The three white members of our party were mounted on stout hill ponies ; and behind us, in Indian file, came about a dozen Assamese natives, who were to act partly as porters and partly as guides and beaters of game. Mr. Marshall accompanied us a little distance on our way, and we parted from him with warm hand-shakes, and many admonitions on his side to be wary and careful of ourselves, and not to overstay long our time.

I am not going to narrate in detail our experiences in the earlier part of the journey, having perhaps already spent too much time in preliminary description, and having much more exciting events to tell of further on. We tried to cover as much ground as possible in the day's march. We were only "provisioned" for three weeks or a month; and it was our desire to get as far into the mountains as possible, and to return within that time. We had little time, therefore, for sport; but occasionally we got a shot at a deer, and twice we thought we saw the striped yellow coat of a tiger slinking through the jungle. On one occasion we suddenly came upon a small herd of wild elephants shampooing one another in a pool in the river; but immediately they caught sight of us they trumpeted loudly, scrambled up the bank, and were crashing their way through the bamboos before we could unsling our rifles and take aim. When we pitched our tent and "went into camp" in the evening, some of us generally turned out with rod and line, and in half an hour would bring in a basket of fine trout, which under Hannibal's skilful hands made a capital addition to our fare. The track we followed for the first few days was one well marked by the feet of elephants, cattle, and natives, generally leading through thick scrub and forest, and keeping near to the banks of the stream that flowed down to the Bramaputra. Often our eyes were unable to penetrate more than a few yards into the depths of the forest, so dense and matted was the wall of trunks and branches woven together by creepers of every size that rose on either side; while overhead the leaves met so closely as almost to shut out the light of the sun even at mid-day. Though the air in these leafy tunnels was close and damp, we were glad to escape the hot glare of the sun that we encountered as soon as we reached the open. We could then see steep rocky banks hemming in the stream we were ascending, and gradually drawing nearer and becoming more precipitous as we advanced. They were still covered with vegetation to the summits; but ahead of us we could see bare and jagged peaks coming into sight, and at night a breeze swept down the valley that felt as if it had blown over snow, and made us glad of the shelter of our tent and blankets. Every mile we advanced the mountains seemed to wrap us more closely in their folds, to take more strange and distorted shapes, and to look down more frowningly on us as trespassers in their domain.

On the sixth day after we had left our bungalow at Poolongyan, we struck off the path we had hitherto been following, and took a more direct cut into the mountains, by a side valley on our right. Dr. Roland, who had carefully studied the lines of the hills and the sketches and accounts of previous travellers, and cross-questioned the native guides, had come to the conclusion that it was in this direction, if anywhere, that a depression in the great snowy range we were in quest of would be found. It was now, however, that the real difficulties of the march began. Regular path there was none, though now and then we could take advantage of well-marked lanes ploughed through the mass of jungle by the heavy bodies of elephants and rhinoceroses, and here and there could trace narrow trails that had apparently been followed by the wild native tribes in their hunting or marauding excursions. We had to send our own elephants to the front to beat down a track through the undergrowth, and our guides had to ply their knives vigorously upon the tough bamboos, lianas, and reeds before we could penetrate the thickets. Often we were compelled to take to the bed of the stream, in which, fortunately, as the dry season had now fairly set in, there was comparatively little water; and elephants, horses, and men scrambled and stumbled over the slippery boulders and ledges in the most uncomfortable way. It was wonderful to see the care and surefooted-ness of our sagacious beasts as they picked their way from rock to rock; but sometimes they would slip down into the stream, and the riders were fortunate if they escaped without bruises, in addition to a wetting. Hannibal was fain to descend from his high station on his elephant's neck, where he was jolted about and torn and lashed with thorns and briers more than he liked, and to pursue the way on foot. For Dr. Roland, however, this part of the journey yielded a rich harvest. His geologist's hammer was constantly in requisition, chipping fragments of the rock, and his note-book, in which he entered the results of his researches, seemed to be seldom long out of his hands. We, of course, flung ourselves with extraordinary ardour into the task of assisting him in the discovery of new plants, insects, and birds. We were so successful, and gained so much praise from our patron, that Hannibal, who appeared to see his scientific functions invaded, while he was doomed to the vulgar duty of looking after the baggage, began to regard us with disdain and perhaps a spice of jealousy. On the whole, however, we were all in high spirits and good-humour. Everything had hitherto gone as smoothly as could be expected, and we had made such good progress that we were already beyond the limits reached by any previous explorer.

The little valley we had been ascending was gradually changing to a gorge. Where we could get a glimpse of the hills above us, we could see great cliffs towering up to meet the sky, with trees and shrubs clinging to the crannies, and trailing plants hanging over the edge of the cliffs and shading them as with a green veil; while overhead huge naked boulders were piled one above

another, and appeared only to wait the first breath of
wind to fall crashing into the valley. In front we could
see where the perpendicular walls closed in, leaving only
a narrow passage between them, and ahead we could
hear the sound of falling waters. Before reaching the
waterfall, however, we had to traverse a sort of canal,
where the stream had an almost imperceptible flow
between marshy banks covered with dense jungle and
forest trees that interlaced their branches and formed a
leafy arcade overhead. Under this gloomy archway,
through which the sun only here and there shot down a
pencil of light, we waded for more than half a mile with
the water nearly to our armpits. The doctor led the
van, holding aloft his rifle and revolver to save them
from the wet, and cautiously piloting the way, which
was full of boulders, deep miry holes, trunks, limbs, and
roots of trees, and other obstacles. Behind him came
the mahout and one of the elephants and the line of
porters, bravely struggling with their loads through the
mud; while Tom and I, leading the ponies, brought up
the rear, along with Hannibal and his big charge, both
of them in rather cross temper, owing to a difference of
opinion as to the rate of progress which it was proper
for an elephant to make in the circumstances. The
worthy old negro's ill-humour was not removed by the
unmerciful chaff to which we subjected him, and a little
incident occurred that threatened further to upset him.

A resplendent butterfly of a new species, with wings four or five inches across, and all ablaze with glorious shades of blue, purple, and crimson, issued from the thicket, and after fluttering round the head of the doctor, who could only vainly shake his revolver at it, it passed on to one after another of the company, finally concentrating its attention on Hannibal, and apparently taking a special delight in parading its beauties within a foot or two of his nose.

"Aha!" said our black friend, wagging his head savagely and showing his teeth like a cat that sees a sparrow from behind a pane of glass, "you t'ink you can do what you like, do you? Hey! You jes' come a little nearah, will you?"

The butterfly, responding to the sarcastic invitation, at that moment danced a few inches closer to Hannibal's face, and by a dexterous sweep of his hand he held the prize in his fingers. Instantly the negro's ill-humour, which was never of long continuance, was appeased, and for the rest of the day he could scarcely conceal the elation he felt. He got his share of the too marked attentions of other tribes of insects—mosquitoes, ants, sand-flies, and the rest—that stung us on the wing or dropped on us from the trees; but he seemed scarcely to mind them. There was not one of us, however, who was not glad enough to emerge again from this damp and dark tunnel into the clear light of day, close beneath the cascade which we had heard gradually sounding louder in our ears.

We were a forlorn company when at length we came to a halt at the foot of the falls. Our hands and faces were torn with thorns and swollen with the stings and bites of our insect tormentors, and our clothes had gaping rents here and there, besides being soaked with water and plastered with mud from the waist down. Hannibal, particularly, cut a bedraggled figure, in melancholy contrast to the spruce and dandified air he assumed before his bright plumage had been drawn through the mire. Tired and wet as we were, hunger had the upper hand of fatigue, and we set to work with a will in helping our cook to get ready our meal—a mess of rice, with preserved meat sandwiches and some excellent crayfish, or "fresh-water lobsters," as we called them, that we had fished up from the stream, added to a smoking cup of tea.

It was a wild scene that environed us as we sat around a great slab of rock, doing ample justice to our fare. Towering granite cliffs rose almost sheer above us to a height of six or seven hundred feet. Piled-up fragments of rock lay around their base and encumbered the bed of the stream, and were overgrown with an extraordinary variety of forest and water plants, among which beautiful ferns and long streaming mosses predominated. On the summit of the crags, also, broken and splintered masses of stone were confusedly heaped, and some of them seemed to lean over in the act of plunging into the valley. We could make out dwarf shrubs clinging to the clefts high up, and hiding behind the boulders, plainly seeking shelter from the cold rude blasts that blew on the plateau above. Just before us the walls of the gorge approached each other within a distance of thirty feet, and down a steep incline rushed the stream in flying leaps and bounds, roaring and chafing over and under the rocks in a line of foam, and falling into a deep pool below. In its present shrunken condition the little river did not nearly fill the space between the cliffs; but in time of flood, as we could plainly see by the markings of water high up the rocks, it must fill the whole channel and thunder through the gap in a resistless torrent.

"What are we to do now, sir?" inquired Tom of the doctor. "We will not be able to get the elephants up these rocks, will we?"

"We must not only leave the elephants behind us," replied our chief, "but also the ponies, if we are to go any further. I am not disappointed about the elephants, as I did not expect to be able to bring them so far. Besides, another day with the care of Ghenghiz weighing on his mind would be the death of Hannibal," glancing slyly at that worthy, who shook his grizzled poll, but looked much relieved. "While you hungry blades have been kindling the fire and boiling the kettle, I have been clambering up the rocks at the fall. There is 'no thoroughfare' that way for horses, and scarcely for foot-passengers. But we have had some experience in climbing trees, and there is a root there by which I find you can hoist yourself up to the river-bed above. I am not quite certain," said the doctor after a pause, and speaking with great deliberation, "but I think I could make out at the extreme end of the gorge, and within a couple of days' march, the great 'divide' of which we are in search."

"Then shouldn't we push on at once?" I broke in.

"Not quite so fast, Bob," said Dr. Roland, smiling at my eagerness. "We have to settle first whether this is not to be our turning-point. We can still spare two or three days and be back at the bungalow by the time appointed. But there is risk, I can see plainly, in pushing on. What if one of the thunderstorms that occasionally break on these hills at this season were to come down? We might be imprisoned in the mountain-gully above for a week or more. It might take that time before the flood would subside sufficiently to let us escape by the fall; and the sides of the gorge, so far as I could observe, are so steep that you might as well think of scaling a church spire. Then there are the hillmen. If they discovered our movements, and chose to bar our way, it would be more awkward even than the floods."

"But we have seen no natives since we crossed the

frontier," we objected, "and those we met within the border were quite quiet and peaceable."

"That sudden disappearance is the very thing that puzzles and troubles me," replied our friend, speaking gravely. . "These wily rascals may have been watching every step we have taken, though they have never allowed us to catch a glimpse of them. Did you observe that the little nât-houses we passed on our way had fresh offerings of fruit and meat laid down to propitiate the evil genii of the jungle and the mountains? The hill-men seldom take the trouble to do that unless some raiding scheme or other mischief is afoot. Now that we are so near the mountains, I think I will push on, with Hannibal and two of the guides, and try to reach the water-parting. But you, boys, must remain here ; or better still, return with the elephants and ponies and the rest of the party to the outlet of the stream, for camping and pasturage. You may look for us in about a week."

The reader may fancy how terribly disappointing a prospect this was for us, and how we urged the doctor by every argument in our power to take us with him. At length, after much hesitation, and bearing in mind that the dangers were, after all, only conjectural, and that we might be safer under his own eye than left alone with the native attendants, he consented that we should start with him next day to pursue the journey up stream.

"I wish you had spent your time, Tom, in teaching your pony to climb trees, instead of standing on its hind legs and begging for a biscuit," said the doctor, looking wistfully at our clever little nags. "We shall have to be the beasts of burden ourselves from this point. I advise you to put on as much clothes as you can bear, and Hannibal will show you how to pack your knapsacks to the best purpose. We must be in as tight marching order as possible, but must have enough food to keep the keen mountain hunger at bay for several days."

CHAPTER III.

THE CLEFTS OF THE ROCK.

LONG before the sun had peeped over the walls of the ravine our preparations for the march were complete. In spite of the wetting of the previous day, we felt quite fresh and fit for travel, thanks partly to the delicious plunge we had enjoyed in the pool immediately on awakening. The critical eyes of the doctor and the "darkey" had superintended every detail of toilet and packing. Elephants, ponies, and attendants stood marshalled, ready for departure to the rear when we had ascended the rocks at the waterfall. Picking our way cautiously over the boulders, wet and slippery with the spray from the cascade, and clinging now to a tuft of grass or fern, now to a root, overhanging branch, or knuckle of rock, we hoisted ourselves up rather stiffly—for we had donned more clothes than was as yet quite comfortable, and had each besides a wallet and a gun slung to his shoulder—till at length we stood on the topmost ledge. We raised a hearty cheer, which was responded to from below; and then each party stepped out briskly, our late companions towards the rendezvous down stream, and we into the unknown heart of the hills.

It is impossible to conceive a more desolate and terrific scene than the one on which our eyes were now turned. A great chasm seemed to have been rent into the core of the mountains, winding and zigzagging, now contracting till it was less than a stone-throw across, and then expanding a little, but with the sheer walls everywhere throwing deep black shadows half-way across the gulf. It seemed to be the gloomy portal to the retreat of the Efreet who guarded the secret of these hills; and it was not strange in young explorers like Tom and myself, who were introduced for the first time into the scenery of this wild land of precipices and abysses, that for a second or two our hearts sank with an involuntary feeling of awe and terror. Above the cliffs that hemmed us in, however, and far back behind the murky recesses of the ravine, a high mountain-ridge could be plainly discerned, running north-east and south-west, with the morning sun gleaming on its snow-covered peaks, and throwing shadows into its deep notches and hollows. We had no doubt that it was the "Iron Wall"—the impassable prolongation of the Patkoi Chain; and it seemed not more than fifteen or twenty miles distant.

The sight infused new spirit into us, and we tramped

on stoutly in spite of obstacles that met us at every step. The bed of the stream was filled with huge blocks of stone, worn smooth with the friction of water passing over them, and piled one above another as if the giants of the hills had been amusing themselves, by trying to fill up the chasm. Our progress was a process of crawling, leaping, sliding, and wading. Sometimes we would be picking our way cautiously along a narrow ledge at a dizzy height above the stream; at others endeavouring to follow its banks by scrambling over the boulders, and then again taking to the stream itself, which hurried downhill in a continuous series of rapids and cataracts. Great fissures seamed the sides of the cliffs at intervals, and side valleys opened up, more dark and forbidding than the main gorge. A coarse wiry grass covered the less steep slopes, and at a few spots there were patches of jungle and forest. We peered anxiously into these thickets, as well as up the branch glens, in search of game or of possible enemies, but saw scarcely any trace of life, human or otherwise. Winged game had disappeared, and the only four-footed creatures we saw were two or three Ovis Ammon, the wild mountain sheep, splendid fellows with prodigious horns, that bounded up the nearly perpendicular crags, and disappeared over the sky-line too far off for us to get a shot at them. The only sport the ravine afforded was angling; and a dish of a curious, snouted, whiting-like fish afforded us an excellent mid-day meal. We could no longer regale ourselves with tropical fruits; for we had left behind us the sago-palm and the rubber-tree, the banyan and the plantain, along with the tiger and the buffalo, in the low valley beneath us, and the plants we now encountered were those of more temperate regions, and chiefly pine-trees not unlike our northern firs.

Still we held onward and upward, and privations and difficulties were made amends for by seeing the snowy range before us grow gradually nearer and clearer. When we halted for the day, we calculated that we had reduced its distance from us by at least one-half. A recess in the rocky wall, with a platform in front commanding a view up and down the ravine, offered a suitable camping-place for the night, and we turned in, after duly setting a watch and kindling a huge fire, satisfied on the whole with what we had done, and prepared to enjoy a well-earned night's repose.

I think the fatigues of the day must have been too much for me, or the cutting breeze that blew down from the snows, and made me shiver within my blanket, prevented me from dropping off to sleep. At all events, I could not compose myself to rest. I heard Dr. Roland and one of the Assamese porters turn in, after having passed the first watch, and Hannibal and our other native follower take their places. The doctor was " dead beat" —for he had been geologizing as well as marching all day

—and did not seem to notice that the two Assam men, willing but superstitious fellows, lingered together for a few moments and exchanged some hurried words. I heard old Han lecturing his companion, with the air of superiority that he always assumed in addressing coloured men of other types than his own, on his ignorance and want of manners.

"You remembah," he said, "a niggah like you ought nevah to speak b'hind the sahib's back. You grumble b'cause you have to climb ovah big stones, and carry other big stones on your back, do you, hey? You don't know that Doctah Sahib"——the doctor's name with the natives—"make dem all into rupees when he goes back to Poolongyan. You 'fraid of the 'nâts,' are you? Why, you fool, he could catch your biggest nât, and cork him up in him small bottle" (this was evidently a blundering allusion to the doctor's splendid collection of gnats and other insects of the same class which he had made one of his specialities). "You jes' keep your eyes well skinned, and mind your own business, will you?"

Much more to the same effect the worthy negro delivered himself of. The Assam man made no response, and Han's own voice sounded drowsily, and at length ceased. The feverish, uneasy sensation I felt was increased by a fancy that I saw a shadow flit past my half-closed eyes towards the entrance of the cave, and by hearing a pebble or two rattle down the rocks outside. I could lie quiet no longer; and besides, I was convinced that the hour was close at hand when Tom and I were to share the morning watch. I got up, and stepped out upon the ledge where our guard was set. The fire had dwindled down until only two or three half-extinct brands remained. The moon had gone down, and the sunrise had hardly begun to tinge the sky. It was indeed the "black hour" that precedes the dawn, and my eyes could only penetrate a few yards into the murky darkness that seemed to surround the dying fire like a wall. There was light enough, however, to see the prostrate figure of Hannibal, stretched close to the embers, and a prolonged snore gave further testimony to the way in which he was keeping watch. It was as I had half suspected. The toils of the day had been too much for the honest fellow, and for once his sense of duty had succumbed to exhaustion.

But where was his companion on guard? I glanced my eye around in search of him, but in vain. Then I stepped aside to see if he had ensconced himself behind some rock. At the instant I moved, an arrow whizzed past, almost brushing my neck, and rattled against a boulder within a few feet of me. For a second or two I felt paralyzed. Then gathering my wits about me, I fired my gun, which I had brought loaded in my hand, in the direction from whence the arrow had come. In-

stantly a howl of pain announced that I had done something more than check the hidden foe and rouse my
companions. The doctor and Tom Wilson rushed out
from the grotto, rifle in hand; and Hannibal picked himself up, and began violently to rub his eyes, evidently
completely at a loss to understand where he was. In a
few hurried words I explained what had happened, and
emphatic point was given to them by two or three other
arrows that came hurtling about us. It was clearly time
to withdraw into the cave; and this we did, after hastily
trampling out the remains of the fire.

Here we lay with our rifles cocked, anxiously waiting
until daylight would break, and spending the interval
in eagerly comparing notes as to the meaning of the
startling event that had occurred, and discussing our
future plans. It was plain that we had fallen into a
trap prepared by a party of the wild hillmen, who may
have been following our trail for days, or perhaps had
been lying in ambuscade in one of the thickets we had
passed on the previous day's march. The disappearance
of both our native porters puzzled us sorely. At first
we suspected complicity on their part with our assailants;
but afterwards we came to the conclusion that they had
been seized with panic, on perceiving the dangers and
difficulties of the enterprise, and had probably overheard some of the doctor's remarks about the likelihood of the dreaded hill-tribes being out upon a raid.

They had seized the first chance of escaping; and we trembled to think of the fate that had overtaken the deserters, and which in a few hours might be our own.

After a weary time of waiting, the objects outside began slowly to loom out more plainly in the darkness, and by-and-by the morning light shone into our place of retreat. The enemy had kept at a respectful distance, and contented themselves with now and again flinging an arrow or lance into the cave from below. We now ventured cautiously to the entrance, and reconnoitred the ground. The besiegers were gathered some distance off in two groups, numbering about twenty men each, one party holding a narrow passage by which alone we could retrace our steps down stream, while the design of the others seemed to be to prevent our pushing further on. They raised an excited yell when they perceived us, and sent a score of arrows in our direction. As we were well sheltered behind the rocks, these did us no harm, and we could survey the foe at comparatively little risk. A more wild, truculent-looking crew surely never gathered together for a deed of rapine or bloodshed. They were rather under the middle height, but with enormously long and powerful limbs. Their faces were of the Mongol type that more or less prevails throughout these hill regions; but in the case of our assailants all the more harsh and sinister features of the Tartar countenance were exaggerated to positive hideousness. Their small, oblique eyes were set underneath a forehead "villanous low;" and their flattened noses, high cheek bones, and wide mouths displaying broken rows of yellow teeth, did not invite the confidence and sympathy of the stranger. Their skins appeared to have once been copper coloured, but abstinence from earliest childhood from the use of soap and water had plastered them with a thick coating of smoke and dirt. Over this repulsive covering they wore a rough garment woven of yak's hair or some other coarse material; their heads were defended by caps of fur or bear-skin, or with great parasol-shaped hats of wickerwork, adorned with yak's tails; and their great splay-feet were bare. For weapons they carried a bow and arrows and spears, and most of them had long-bladed knives stuck in their belts.

Seeing that we made no movement, they began to shout to us in harsh, guttural tones, and indulged in an insulting pantomime, obviously daring us to come forth and meet them. One rascal held aloft a tin saucepan— one of Hannibal's most cherished possessions—which he had pilfered from the neighbourhood of the fire, and brandished it in triumph. This was too much for the negro, who was bringing his rifle to bear on the thief, when the doctor struck up the barrel.

"Don't fire one of you till I give the word," he said, for Tom and I were also fingering our triggers. "Just think what a terrible thing it is to take the life of a human being, however degraded. We must beware of exasperating them, until we are sure that there is no way of escape except by fighting; and, remember, in our present case every cartridge is worth to us a king's ransom."

Again the trophy was flourished in the air; and the enemy, who had evidently no idea of the range of our weapons, advanced a few paces nearer. The doctor, a splendid shot, brought his rifle to his shoulder, took a steady aim, and fired. The saucepan, from which Hannibal had in his time produced some of the greatest triumphs of the cooking art, dropped from the hands of the astonished savage, a hole being driven clean through the bottom of it, and after a second or two of comical confusion, he and his companions fled in dismay. At the pass below, however, they rallied, ashamed of their panic. Afraid of venturing to close quarters, they now disposed themselves behind rocks and shrubs, so as to command every yard of our path of retreat, and seemed to have adopted the tactics of starving us into surrender.

It was now time to decide on a plan of extricating ourselves; and the circumstances seemed indeed desperate. We waited, of course, for our chief's directions.

"There is just one way open for us, boys," he said, in a cheery, hopeful voice. "We cannot force that gateway with so many yelling savages guarding it; we cannot

climb up these sheer walls of rock; and it is plain we
cannot remain where we are, with only a couple of days'
food with us. The path ahead is not obstructed; we
have cleared it at the cost of Hannibal's frying-pan."

"And berry dear cost, too," grumbled that personage,
glancing ruefully at the ruined cooking-vessel. "How
am I to cook your dinnah when you go knock de
bottom out dat pan, sar?"

"We'll better settle how we are to get any dinner to
cook," answered the doctor dryly. "But there is no
time to lose. Get ready everything we must take along
with us: cartridges and food first, then clothes; leave
saucepans and luxuries of that kind to their fate, and—
quick march! Somewhere between this and the top of
the gorge we shall surely find some spot where young,
active legs can scramble up to the plateau above, and so
back to the friends we have left in the valley behind,—
especially when we have flights of poisoned arrows to
hasten our steps.—Bob, my lad," he added more gravely,
looking critically at one of the arrows, as we resumed
our march up stream, "you have had a very narrow
escape. A slight prick from this would have left you
with a very short lease of life."

As we proceeded, our persecutors left their intrenched
positions and cautiously followed in our wake, taking
care to keep well out of range of our rifles. There was
another remarkable change in our surroundings, for the

granite rocks gave place to stupendous cliffs of limestone formation, and the scenery seemed to grow more weird and fantastic every minute. The river had worn its bed into deep ruts and basins, hollowing out for itself yawning archways and caverns in the rock, or leaving strangely-carved blocks standing in mid-stream. The face of the cliffs was honeycombed with caves. White stalactites hung from the roofs and glimmered in the obscurity with a ghostly effect. Above towered the similitude of feudal castles, with ruined turrets and tottering walls, decaying minsters with needle-pointed spires and flying buttresses, columns, obelisks, and towers of every strange outline, all standing sharply defined against the sky. It would scarcely have surprised us if a train of hunch-backed manikins, like the trolls, gnomes, and kobolds we had been reading of in German fairy stories, had issued from one of these darkling caves, bending under the weight of the great sacks of gold and precious stones that they carried on their shoulders. It was with a kind of shudder that we fancied we saw movements in the depths of the grottoes, as of shadowy things flitting to and fro,—doubtless some of the large vampire bats, the capture of which had been one of the main objects that had lured the doctor into the mountains.

But to-day we were in no mood either for geologizing or making notes on natural history, and we pushed on with all the speed we could muster. No breach, however, opened up in the prison walls that hemmed us in, offering a portal to liberty and safety. There was no foothold on the cliffs which even a goat could take advantage of as a ladder of escape. Instead, the crags towered above us on either hand more threateningly and steeply than before, and in front also vast precipices, surmounted by seemingly unscalable heights, barred our way; for we had now arrived close to the base of the mountain-chain we had come so far to see. The skies also seemed to frown on our enterprise, for great clouds were gathered overhead, and the air in the confined gorge was close and suffocating. Our pursuers seemed to perceive that our hour had come, for they uttered a shout of triumph as they crept nearer, skilfully taking advantage of the enormous masses of rock that had slipped down into the gorge and obstructed our way, but which their bare feet easily surmounted.

Suddenly we saw them stop, glance at the sky, and hastily take shelter in the clefts of the rock near them. At the same moment a deep shadow appeared to fall on us, and looking up, the heavens overhead seemed covered with a black, sulphurous-looking pall, rolled fold within fold, and gradually being drawn down closer upon us.

"Run—run, lads, for your lives!" said Dr. Roland, and seizing an arm apiece of Tom and me, he hurried us at the top of our speed to the mouth of a cave which opened a friendly refuge close at hand.

Hannibal followed on our heels; and hardly had we ensconced ourselves within when the skies appeared to open, and a great blaze of white light of exceeding vividness illuminated the gloomy gorge to its innermost recesses, followed instantaneously by a terrific crash of thunder, that seemed to echo and re-echo from every cleft and cavern in the mountains. Flash followed flash, and peal succeeded peal with stunning rapidity, and great hailstones, or rather blocks of ice, as large, or larger, than a pigeon's egg, began to fall, first hopping and dancing fantastically among the rocks, whirling madly round in an eddying wind that came sweeping down the gullies, and then, as the gusts increased in strength, tearing along in solid battalions, lashing wildly the sides of the cliffs, and battering us even in the shelter of the cave with the hard jagged particles. After the hail came sleet; and then rain descended in great sheets, and continued for an hour and a half, amid the almost incessant crashing and rumbling of the thunder.

While this tremendous concert was proceeding, we looked on breathless and awe-stricken, hardly daring to exchange a word with one another. Indeed, it would not have been easy to have made ourselves heard amidst the pealing of the thunder, the howling of the wind, and the roar of many waters; for the stream, which a little before was a mere brook, had become a powerful torrent, that chafed like a netted lion among the rocks, and was reinforced every few yards by streams that tumbled down the gullies in lines of foam, or cascades that precipitated themselves over the edge of the cliffs.

Just as the storm seemed to be expending its fury in a last burst, a new and more terrifying sound struck upon our ears. The solid mountain shook and trembled beneath us, and a loud and long-resounding crash seemed to announce that the world was falling in ruins. Even the doctor's cheek blanched, I fancied, for an instant; and the thought that occurred to all our minds was that we had experienced one of the shocks of earthquake not uncommon in Assam.

Almost immediately the rain ceased, and the sun appeared to be struggling through the clouds; but the air was obscured by thick dust that filled the valley. When this had cleared away, we at once perceived what had happened. An extensive landslip had occurred between us and the spot where we had seen our savage foes seek shelter. A huge mass of the mountain had toppled over into the gorge, completely blocking it, with the exception of a narrow gap through which the pent-up waters of the stream were rushing. Passage over this obstacle there was none. At length we were safe from pursuit—if, indeed, our pursuers had not been buried under the falling mountain.

We could not afford to wait long musing over the

singular manner in which we had been released from
the more immediate danger. Other perils not less formidable encompassed us. So far as could be seen, we
were shut up in the heart of a mountain, as in a kind
of well, surrounded by frightful precipices on all sides,
and a hundred miles from the nearest outpost of civilization. Our first care, of course, was to search for some
point where the cliffs would be found accessible. If we
failed in this, nothing less than death from starvation
stared us in the face. The afternoon was already advanced, and with our almost exhausted supplies no time
was to be lost. At first it seemed as if we were to be
balked in every attempt to escape from our prison in
the clefts of the rock. Many fissures branched off from
the head of the gorge, but all alike ended in terrific
precipices. We turned back from the last of them, tired
out and almost despairing.

"What have you got there, Hannibal?" asked Tom
of the negro, who had stooped and picked up an object
from the ground. "Something to eat, I hope."

"Don't know I'm sure, Massa Tom," was the reply.
"'Pears to be a bit of hoop, but might once have been a
cutlass."

The doctor took the rusty piece of iron from Hannibal's hands, and examined it long and narrowly.

"This is important, boys," he said. "It means that
other travellers have been here before us. It is a knife-

blade of Burmese manufacture. I have often heard that the Shans from the Upper Irrawady cross the mountains, and barter these knives, and also metal ornaments and cloth, with the hill-tribes, in exchange for furs, musk, medicinal plants, yak's hair, and other productions of the mountains. It is plain that a road leads past this spot; and if barbarians can follow it merely for trade, I think Britons need not shrink from it in a matter of life and death. Let us go back and look again."

We raised a hearty cheer at this good news. Fortune seemed resolved to smile on us in our extremity; for our shout startled an antelope that had taken cover behind a rock near at hand, and it dashed in a slanting line up the cliffs. The doctor's rifle was instantly at his shoulder, but to our surprise he did not fire, contenting himself with covering the animal's body as it bounded along the precipitous face of the crags.

"Fire, doctor!—fire, or it will be gone!" called Tom with his accustomed headlong eagerness.

The doctor, however, took his time; but at last the report of the gun awakened the echoes of the hills, and the antelope, after a desperate effort to maintain its foothold, fell from a great height, crashing from rock to rock, till it lay motionless at the bottom.

"I wished to watch the track it took," explained the doctor, as Hannibal shouldered the body and we turned away. "And now I think I have the clue that will lead us out of this trap."

That night we supped cheerfully on roast haunch of venison, and I think that, in spite of the lamented loss of our cooking apparatus, the whole party enjoyed a meal so plentifully sauced with hunger—except myself.

CHAPTER IV.

THE IRON WALL.

NOT only did I not relish supper, but I passed another night of feverish restlessness, and in the morning I felt quite ill. The fact was that I was suffering from the first symptoms of fever, that I had doubtless caught in our wade through the marshes below. I knew, however, that the lives of myself and my companions depended on our getting out of our present position with all speed; and I saw plainly in Dr. Roland's face, in spite of his cheerful tone, that he was keenly reproaching himself for having been the means of bringing us into such deadly peril. I resolved, therefore, to bear up to the last gasp, rather than add to his anxiety, or be a burden to my comrades.

We began the ascent of the mountain, following as closely as possible the steps of the antelope we had shot, the doctor leading the way, and I bringing up the rear, where my companions had least chance of noticing my distress. I have a very confused and vague remembrance of the events of this notable day. I cannot describe the features of the Iron Wall, and I could not lead a party over it. This, however, is of small consequence, as its wonders, with the particulars regarding the nature of its rocks and its plant and animal life, will be fully dealt with in Dr. Roland's great work of travel and discovery. I only know that, slowly and painfully, we scrambled our way upwards to the region of cloud and snow. We crawled like flies along the flank of the mountain, treading narrow ledges where a single false step would have been destruction, clinging desperately to rock and root, and stepping across yawning fissures that made the head swim as we peered fearfully into their depths. Grass and shrubs gave place to Alpine mosses and lichens or naked rocks, and patches of snow lay in the sheltered spots. There was urgent need that we should cross the " divide " before nightfall; for if we slept out on the bare mountain-side we ran the risk of being frozen to death, or if a storm like that of the previous day overtook us we should be blown into space like straws. It was impossible to move a yard aside from our path, girded in as it was by precipices; and we noticed many signs—notches and steps cut in the rock, and occasionally the trunk of a tree laid across a crevasse—that proved that the way had been traversed by others before us. It led to a deep " saddle," which we now saw in the ridge above us, some fifteen hundred feet, as near as we could judge, below the snowy peaks on either side.

For myself, I despaired of ever reaching this goal of our desires. My fingers trembled and my knees knocked together as I crept along the dizzy ledges, and a film gathered before my eyes as I strove to keep pace with my companions. An ague fit made my teeth chatter as I tried to set them and keep in a cry for help, and the wind from the frozen heights above pierced me like an icicle. Latterly I think I must have fallen into a half-insensible state, and struggled on mechanically with the strength of delirium. We had climbed high above the level of the lower hills, and a majestic panorama of mountain and valley was spread below us. It seemed as if in a dream I were being carried, by no will of my own, up the steep slope of a colossal wave, with a tempestuous sea of white-crested billows heaving and falling around me, and unfathomable black gulfs opening up between.

At last nature gave way, and I sank down helpless on the track. My comrades moved on some paces before they observed what had befallen me, and then in an instant they were all about me. I remember feebly urging them to leave me to my fate, and to hurry forward for their own safety. The doctor felt my pulse, and prepared a draught from the little medicine-box that he always carried about with him, speaking cheerfully and affectionately as I endeavoured to swallow it; and my dear friend Tom grasped my other hand, while tears gathered in his eyes. Then Hannibal hoisted me tenderly upon his brawny shoulders—fortunately I was a light weight, and sturdy Tom would have been a much more serious burden—and the up-hill march was resumed as I lapsed into unconsciousness.

For a second or two I "came round," and opening my eyes found myself supported by my companions, and surrounded by deep snow, with icy peaks rising on either hand. The sun was going down behind us, and threw gigantic shadows on the mists that were gathering below; and the snowy ridges that I had fancied were white-crested waves now looked like icebergs floating in a lake of purple. In front of us, however, there was an opening in the clouds, and a glimpse was caught of a deep defile like that which we had left behind us, opening in the distance into a larger valley, where there was the far-off gleam of rushing waters.

The doctor was finishing some remark, and I caught the word "Irrawady." I had my wits sufficiently about me to understand that we had reached the crisis of victory—that we had surmounted the great barrier, and discovered the hidden upper course of the great river of Burmah. I waved my hand, and uttered a feeble "Hurrah."

"Hurrah!" echoed Tom in a voice that struggled to be firm, and then the whole "expedition" cheered in chorus.

CHAPTER V.

UPS AND DOWNS.

WHEN I came again to my senses I was lying in a cave, on a comfortable couch of fir branches, covered with skins of deer and bear. For a moment or two I imagined that I had never left the grotto where we had slept on the night after we had parted from the bulk of our followers at the falls, and that all that had happened since —the desertion of our guides, the attack and pursuit of the savages, the thunderstorm, and the perilous journey over the mountain—was a nightmare dream. The cliffs that I caught glimpses of through the entrance of the cave had the same fantastic shapes that had become familiar to us on the other side of the Iron Wall, and rose into slender spires and pinnacles, flanked with turrets and overhanging eaves that seemed to put the laws of gravity at defiance. But as I propped myself upon my elbow and noted this, I perceived that there was an important change from the scenes I had left. The valley was

wider, its walls were higher, and the whole features of the
landscape were on a grander scale. That we were in a
warmer climate, too, was evident from the half-tropical
plants that draped the entrance to the cave, and clung
to the nooks and crannies of the rocks; while above,
great pine forests began, and stretched almost to the
summit of the hills. I tried to sit up, in order to get
a better view, but was glad to fall back again upon
the fur pillows, and bear with what patience I could the
affliction of waiting for an explanation.

I had not long to wait. In a few minutes the honest
black face of Hannibal appeared at the mouth of the
cave. He stepped in upon tiptoe; but when he saw
my eyes wide open and staring inquiringly at him, he
gave a start, half of fright and half of joy, as if he were
about to jump out of his skin, and hurried up to me.

"Oh, golly, Massa Bob!" he said, seizing my hand,
while two big tears rolled down the sides of his nose,
as if racing each other to reach the tip—"you have got
frew it?"

"Through what, Han?" I replied, for my ideas were
still somewhat confused. "Have we come right through
below the mountain?"

Before Han could reply the doctor and Tom entered,
and were, of course, not less overjoyed to see that the
fever had left me. From the three I gradually got
explanations of what had happened since I lost con-

sciousness on the mountain-top. To my surprise I heard
that a whole fortnight had elapsed since then, during
which time my companions more than once feared that
they would lose me. The descent of the mountain, they
assured me, had been comparatively easy. A glacier
ran a long way down into the valley, and taking advantage of the hard-pressed snow that lay upon it, they
had constructed a kind of sleigh, with a brake contriv-
ance to regulate the speed, such as the doctor had seen
in operation in Canada and Russia, and slid rapidly and
easily down to the region of pine forests. The passage
was a dangerous one, for any moment a crevasse might
have opened and swallowed us; but there was no other
way of descent, and we arrived safely at the bottom.
From thence my comrades had carried me by easy stages
to the spot where I now lay, within hearing of the
rushing flood of the Irrawady. They made light of the
toils that I had caused them by so inopportunely
breaking down; but I knew what unspeakable cause
for thankfulness I had to them for so bravely sticking
by me, and so tenderly nursing me in my delirium and
weakness. Afterwards I had chances of paying a small
part of my debt of gratitude; for before our journey
ended, we had all had our share of fever, and had each
our turns of being nurse and patient.

During my fever fit, and while I was recovering
strength, my comrades were not idle. The doctor was

out on the hills every day, accompanied either by Tom
or Hannibal, surveying the ground, hunting, or collecting
scientific information; while one of the party was left
"at home," as we learned to call our cave, to attend to
the sick and to the cooking.   Fortunately game was not
scarce, and many a fragrant stew Hannibal prepared,
by the aid of our last preserved-meat tin, with the
pheasants, wild duck, quail, and deer that made up the
daily bag; while the river yielded a welcome change of
fare, especially when we were lucky enough to hook the
lordly mahseer, a fish as large and as fine-flavoured—at
least such was the opinion of one hungry convalescent—
as the salmon.   Pot vegetables, edible mushrooms, salads,
and other garnishing were not wanting—for here the
doctor's botanical knowledge came very usefully to our
aid; and we soon learned to like the wild rhubarb which
grew plentifully on the higher ground.   For dessert we
laid under contribution the fine walnut, chestnut, apricot,
peach, and cherry trees that covered the slopes of the
gorges, as well as the brambles, wild gooseberries, straw-
berries, and rasps that throve in the covers below; so
that altogether we were, in respect to food, not greatly
to be pitied, in spite of the doses of *tete* and other
indigenous drugs which the doctor made us swallow
daily as a precaution against fever.

We could not, however, live for ever in this secluded
valley, and our main subject of anxiety was our future

route. A careful survey of the ground had shown that there was no escape by the river, either up or down stream. About two miles above us the Irrawady narrowed to little more than a dozen yards, and tore with a sound like thunder down a series of cataracts, between sheer walls of rocks rising to a height of many hundreds of feet. At a distance of a few hundred yards below us the stream entered another gorge, scarcely so steep and narrow—for fine larch and fir trees partly clothed the face of the cliffs, and rose tier above tier till they seemed dwindled to shrubs—but equally impassable either by land or water. Nearly opposite us was a reach of comparatively calm water; and at no great distance off, on the other bank, the entrance to a side valley, similar to the one we had descended, promised us the only loophole of escape. Plenty of logs and brushwood was scattered along the shore, left there by the summer floods, which we noticed marked a rise of forty or fifty feet in the river-level in the confined channels above and below. Out of this material it was easy to construct a raft; and as another fortnight's rest had made me feel strong enough to resume the march, we embarked one fine morning on this cumbrous craft; and after half-an-hour's hard toil, and several narrow escapes from going to pieces on the rocks, or being swept down by the current and eddies, we managed to reach safely the opposite bank.

Landing, and shouldering our knapsacks, which we had taken care to store with what was needful for several days' march through a sterile and probably uninhabited country, we allowed our raft to drift away down stream, where it was soon tossing and whirling among the rapids.

Then the doctor made us a little speech.

"It is six weeks, as you know, boys," he said, "since we left our friends at Poolongyan. We were due to return there a fortnight ago; but instead, we have been drifting, like that raft there, further and further away, into wilder and more troubled scenes, with no possibility of return by the way we have come. We must now make up our minds about what we are to do; and I say that we must turn our backs upon India and make China our aim. We have made one great discovery— though chance, rather than design, has led us to it. Others as wonderful lie ahead; and it will be a noble ambition to make them ours. In the first place, we have to climb these hills; and I hope that we shall shortly reach the valley of the Salwen river, where we shall be able to purchase mules at some of the tribal villages or at a Buddhist monastery; for, you know, we are going up into Thibet, and there the priests are the kings. You must be prepared to meet dangers and hardships— more than I would ever have dreamed of exposing you to, if I had known where our trip would have led us.

We shall probably have to face wild beasts and robbers, precipices and torrents, cold and hunger; but I do not see why, with stout hearts and limbs, and clear heads and consciences, and with weapons to fill our larder, and in a last extremity to defend our lives, we should not come through them all. We choose to consider ourselves as explorers, not as fugitives, and cheery endeavour will be our watchword."

" ' Be not like dumb, driven cattle,
Be a hero in the strife,' "

chimed in Tom, swinging a tough oak cudgel he had cut to assist his steps. So it was to the words of Long-fellow's beautiful " Psalm of Life " that we began the toilsome ascent of the Thibetan mountains; and I think if you could have watched us as we stepped out, you would have said that there was some of its fire in our eyes and our hearts.

It was not long before we had to make large demands on our stock both of courage and of patience. I fear it might weary my readers to have a daily record of our arduous journey among the bare and savage mountains through which our route now led us for many days. I can assure them that in actual fact it was much more wearisome than it could possibly be made in description. They may get some small idea of the mere fatigue that had to be undergone, if they can find a staircase six thousand feet high or more, and climb to the top of it every morning and down again every night. But even this would not take account of the terrors and the perils of the way. The slippery ledges along which we had to pick our steps, and where a crumbling fragment of the rock disturbed by the foot would bound down for hundreds of feet into the gloomy ravine, its distant splash lost in the boom of rushing waters, brought us to snowy ridges, on which, after all our toilsome climbing, we dared not rest, so piercing was the cold, and so rarefied the air in which we sought in vain to fetch back our spent breath. Then we had to scramble down steep slopes, torn into deep ruts and covered with splinters of slaty rock, as if some huge harrows had been dragged athwart the hills, until we found ourselves in the gloomy depths of a ravine, where only a thin slip of blue sky was to be seen overhead. At mid-day our faces would be cracked and blistered by the frosty winds that blew on the mountains; and ere nightfall the close, sultry air of the confined valleys almost stifled us. With all our exertions we seemed to make no progress. The gorge where, for the sake of warmth and shelter, we would halt for the evening was an exact model of the one we had left in the morning. When the new barrier of precipitous mountain had been painfully climbed, the top disclosed more heights, snowy, bare, or pine-covered, rising in front of us.

It must not be thought, however, that there was no

beauty or grace in these savage scenes. Often the route carried us over grassy hills and hollows, where, in spots sheltered from the powerful sun, the sward was thickly sown with daisies, buttercups, and less familiar flowers, whose names and properties the doctor took care to explain to us. We were sure to meet with slopes covered with rhododendrons, camellias, azaleas, and other plants with glossy green leaves and bright blossoms, and to pass through forests of tall firs, cedars, and larches, before coming to the cold, bare heights above.

But gradually, as we advanced, the features of the scenery grew more harsh and abrupt; the gaunt bones of the mountains pushed themselves further through their turfy covering, until only thin patches of green checkered the sterile rocks. Game, too, failed us. The daily "bag" dwindled down until it no longer yielded us a satisfying meal at the close of the march. Hunger began to vex us. We were constantly coming upon signs of the wandering tribes of savages that haunt these hills, in the shape of embers of camp-fires and remains of temporary huts. The track we were following was evidently often used by them, and some of their hunting parties had passed over it only a little time before. At first we had congratulated ourselves at not falling in with such dangerous wayfarers; but we now began to wish that we would light upon a living creature of any sort whatsoever mute or loud. Were it the latter, it might serve us for a meal: if the former, we might be served in our turn; but any risk seemed better than the certainty of starvation from cold and hunger.

On the fifth evening after we had crossed the Irrawady, we halted for the night in a small grove of forest trees.   In truth, so "dead beat" were we that we could not have dragged our tired limbs many yards further, and we were glad to take advantage of the shelter the trees afforded.   To add to our misery, our last scrap of food had been eaten, and to-night, for the first time, we must go supperless to bed.

"Hallo!" said Tom, stretching himself below one of the trees, "if this isn't a holly! Doesn't it remind one of Christmas-time at home—roast-beef, plum-pudding, and all the rest?"

"Please don't speak of roast-beef and plum-puddin', Massa Tom," said poor Hannibal, the cook, pleadingly. "It hurts my feelin's."

"And please don't speak of hollies, Master Tom, when you should say oaks," put in the doctor.

"Why, this is a holly, is it not, sir?" Tom rejoined. "Look at these leaves—and the prickles," he added, hastily withdrawing his hand, for he had allowed one of the sharp spines to run into his finger.

"But look at the height, and the bark, and more particularly the acorns," retorted Dr. Roland.   "It is the holly-leaved oak of Thibet, Tom, and wiser men than you have been deceived by it."

"Let us camp under one of them," I suggested. "It will be a double reminder of England and good cheer."

"Both dearer for their absence," murmured Tom.

So we selected one of these strange, bushy oak trees, that promised to give us effectual shelter, and soon were seated around a crackling fire of dry fir branches.

"Is there nothing left in the pantry at all, Hannibal?" asked the doctor; "not even twice-used tea leaves, to make a brew of?"

"No, sar," replied Han sadly, at the same time producing from his pockets and laying before the embers some ripe chestnuts that he had knocked down from the trees with stones while we had been discussing the holly *versus* oak question.

There was little opportunity to-night for renewing the loving squabble that we had every meal-hour over the division of the food, in which each manœuvred to get the largest shares for his neighbours. I am afraid Hannibal told terrible fibs about the quantities he consumed while cooking, in order to excuse his small appetite when his dishes were produced. The doctor was deaf to the arguments of Tom and myself, that being a big full-grown man, he ought to have double the share of us lads. It was the same at bedtime: the question of the party were continually quarrelling for the most uncomfortable post, or heaping clothes about those who were "caught napping." Then, on the march, I hardly knew whether to cry for vexation or for gratitude at the way my companions persisted in treating me as still an invalid, who ought to be relieved of hard work as much as possible. It is incredible the dodges by which that rascal Tom—generally the most frank, straightforward fellow breathing—would try to get possession of my gun, and insist on carrying it for me. As was only our duty, every one tried now and throughout the journey to keep up as contented, manly, and even "jolly" a demeanour as he could, for the sake of his comrades; but each must have felt that the situation was becoming desperate. So we cheered the appearance of the handful of chestnuts, though, for myself, I felt so hungry that I could have sat down prepared to do justice to a leg of elephant.

"What will happen to us to-morrow, sir?" asked some of us of the doctor.

"I would not like to prophesy," he replied, "but I think that we must be near the crisis of our troubles. From the distance we have marched, we must be quite close to the basin of the Salwen. For the first time, we have found no gorge between the ranges, only a hollow. I shouldn't wonder if, when we crest the hill in front of us, we should see both the river and the savages. They have apparently hunted all the game from this side of the watershed, and have followed to the banks of the Salwen. Or, perhaps, they have been northward on a raid, and are now seeking shelter from the Thibetan troops in their remotest gorges."

From Thibet and its snows and savages our discourse gradually turned, as it was always sure to do, to the little island in the northern seas which we so proudly claimed as our country; and we talked long of our friends at home, and how small idea they could have of our strange surroundings. The night had fallen, and the keen frosty air made us shiver; for our camping-ground was higher than any we had yet reached, and our clothes, ill-suited in any case for such an arctic climate, were torn by thorns and rocks. So we crept up close to the fire, and heaped on more fuel, till the smoke curled in great clouds through the branches above us.

All at once we were astounded by a violent shaking of the boughs overhead and a monstrous black apparition gradually descending almost into our midst. First appeared a shapeless mass, covered with long shaggy black hair, hanging from a lower limb of the tree; and then shoulders and fore paws, and lastly a snouted head emerged into sight, as with angry gruntings the creature leisurely descended the trunk. So surprised were we that it was a few seconds before we could realize that we were   on the intruded by a mountain bear, who had probably climbed the tree to feast on the acorns, and had remained hidden in the thick foliage and failing light, until we had "smoked" him off his perch. Our guns were piled behind the tree, and the doctor had barely time to slip round and seize his rifle, when his bearship was among us. He seemed in a shockingly bad humour, for he growled angrily and champed his great jaws together, as, still half-blinded with the smoke, he blundered forward into the fire, scattering the lighted brands in all directions, and, I am bound to admit, putting us ignominiously to flight. By this time the doctor had got his gun ready, and fired; but a branch catching his sleeve, the bullet only grazed Bruin's cheek, and enraged him the more. He turned and made again towards the tree, but a smart blow over the nose from Hannibal with a burning fagot made him change his mind; and after a struggle between wrath and prudence, he shuffled off into the darkness.

It did not, however, suit hungry travellers to see a possible supper disappear in this manner; so, taking our guns, we started in search. It is not altogether pleasant to hunt for an angry bear in a dark wood; and I own that my heart jumped to my mouth when, coming round the trunk of a tree, I felt a hot breath in my face, and saw a shadowy shape, that seemed of gigantic dimensions, within a yard or two of me. For the second time that night I fled with the bear close at my heels; but luckily the doctor was close at hand, and a shot through the brain bowled over my slouching pursuer. By-and-by we were feasting joyously on bear-steaks; and I am in a position to say that for desperately hungry men, and when there is nothing better to be had, they are not to be despised.

CHAPTER VI.

THE VALLEY OF THE SHADOW.

NEXT morning we breakfasted on Bruin, and resumed the march. Bearing in mind the likelihood of the savages being near at hand, we thought it proper to move with circumspection; so, instead of following the track that would have carried us directly over the ridge in front, we proceeded southward some distance down the valley that ran parallel to it, and then climbed cautiously to the top, and peered over, under the shelter of a great rock. What we saw entirely satisfied us of the correctness of the doctor's views as to our whereabouts, and of the wisdom of the precautions we had taken not to expose ourselves. Before us were short ranges of hills, separated by narrow valleys, and all running in the same general direction—north and south—as those we had already crossed, but so much lower than that on which we stood, that we could make out beyond them what appeared to be a long deep furrow ploughed through the mountains. This could hardly be other than the long-looked-for gorge of the Salwen river. On the other side were more lines of hills, rising step behind step to a snowy range, with the sun glistening on its peaks.

But what chiefly attracted our notice was the scene that lay directly at our feet. A kind of natural amphitheatre was hollowed in the hill, and completely enclosed by two spurs thrown off from the range. The only openings from it were a pass at the upper end, that we should have traversed if we had pursued the direct route, and a narrow rocky gorge below, by which a small stream escaped to the Salwen. The rocks where we stood descended almost perpendicularly, and you could fancy that you could drop a stone upon a grassy flat extending on each bank of the rivulet below, though it must have been almost a quarter of a mile away. On this piece of turf a singular-looking group was gathered. We almost fancied that we recognized our acquaintances who had hunted us so persistently a few weeks ago. The features, the gestures, the costume, and the weapons —so far as we could make them out from our lofty station—generally resembled those of the Assam hillmen ; but these people seemed to have come less into contact with civilized ways than even their brethren on the western side of the Iron Wall. Some of them were clad in th. .... f. .nament what app ... . .1 their necks, and large earrings dangling on their shoulders; but others had no covering from the cold beyond a waistcloth and their long black hair. We fancied we could make out tattoo-marks on their limbs and chests. Groups of sheep, goats, and small, shaggy-coated horses and mules were pasturing on the grass, and the deep baying of several huge yellow dogs came up to us. But the most curious-looking objects were a score or so of immense hairy beasts, like enormous goats, yet with something about them reminding one of domestic cattle, that quietly fed among the other animals. They had down-looking heads, short muzzles, and humps like bisons; a long fell of hair descended from their dew-laps and flanks almost to the ground, and their tails were huge bunches of white or brown hair. A little reflection, of course, told Tom and me that this must be the famous yak, the domestic ox of Thibet; but Hannibal was sorely puzzled, and one could see, from his nervous glances in their direction, that rather than face one of these mysterious-looking creatures, he would encounter a dozen of savages.

Smoke curled up from the valley, and preparations were going on for a feast as we stood discussing in low tones what steps we should take. One of the yaks was led out into an open space, and, apparently at a given signal, one of the men sprang upon it with the bound of a panther, and plunged a long knife into its throat,

Instantly the whole savage crew flung themselves on
the struggling beast, and cut and slashed and hacked
off great pieces of flesh with sickening ferocity.   The
sight was not one to inspire us with confidence; but
feeling it necessary to be doing something, and fearing
that we would be caught sight of by the group below,
we began to move towards the pass, carefully keeping
ourselves concealed behind the brow of the hill.   We
had not gone far when we noticed an unusual movement in the camp of the savages.   They seemed to have
suspended their meal, and to be hastily preparing for
flight.   Looking back into the valley we had left, we at
once saw the cause of the commotion.   A cavalcade had
emerged from the hills, and was already crossing the
shallow stream we had waded on the previous night.
The hillmen had evidently scouts posted on the pass,
who had given them notice of the approach of danger.

The new-comers drew nearer, and it would be difficult
to imagine a more motley group.   Some of the party
were on foot, but the majority were mounted on horses
or on yaks, while a train of pack-mules and donkeys
brought up the rear.   The objects of the company
seemed to be partly military and partly trading; for
while most of them carried long spears, and here and
there the stock of an old flintlock showed itself, others
were atti... the p...... ... r.....   Th... r.. was the
same var..ty in f......... and d...... as in martial equip-

THE VALLEY OF THE SHADOW.

ment. Bold, harsh, Tartar traits and rough sheep-skin garments predominated, but there were several members of the party whose regular features, full, flowing beards, and ample robes and turbans recalled the Mohammedan races of Western Asia.

We had not long time for deliberation, and Dr. Roland at once decided that we should show ourselves. The appearance of four men—three of them white and one intensely black—suddenly starting up from among the rocks, caused unbounded surprise and not a little consternation. Seeing, however, how small our party was, the strangers quickly recovered from their panic, and several barrels were levelled at us. The doctor at once made signs of amity, and shouted something in Chinese to the leader of the band, who evidently understood him, for after a short parley we were signalled to approach. Our new acquaintances, we found, were a party of horse who had been sent out to punish a raid which the Lu-tzes, a notorious tribe of robbers, had made into Thibetan territory, and, if possible, to recover the plunder. Along with them were several traders from Kashgar, who, we learned, had travelled across the breadth of Thibet with their wares, and had seized this chance of getting an escort across the wild, unsettled country between them and the Chinese mart of Tali-fu, to which they were bound.

The captain of the Thibetans was a tall, stalwart

fellow, with a fierce black eye, and restless, energetic
movements, who was only distinguished from his followers by the greater profusion of coral and turquoise
ornaments about him, and by the jade-hilted sword stuck
in his belt. He seemed greatly puzzled to know what to
do with us; for the lamas—the priestly rulers of Thibet
—have an inveterate objection to strangers, and especially Englishmen, entering their sacred country. The
doctor, however, rightly judged of the kind of arguments
that the Kashgaree merchants must have used to overcome this prejudice; and after a short chat with the
leader, in which we distinctly heard the clink of some
of the Indian rupees which pass freely current in
Thibet, we were allowed to join the band.

Our new friends were astonished when they heard
from us that the marauders of whom they were in
pursuit were so close at hand, and hastened forward
with all speed to overtake them; but when we came in
sight of the green basin in the mountain, where a few
minutes before we had seen so animated a sight, it
was quite empty. Savages, yaks, mules, horses, sheep,
and dogs had disappeared, as if the hill had opened and
swallowed them up. I rubbed my eyes, and felt like
one of those belated travellers who have watched a fairy
pageant until the whole of the little green-jerkined company have vanished at cockcrow; or like Fitz-James when
"Clanalpine's warrior" sank from sight at the beck of

Roderick Dhu. Our Thibetan guard probably did not trouble their minds with such fancies; for they instantly set spurs to their horses, and went clattering down the glen, over rock and hillock, at a great rate, leaving us foot-passengers far behind.

By-and-by from the gorge below came sounds of battle—shots that echoed and echoed again among the hills, hoarse shouts and words of command, the deep lowing of yaks, the neighing of horses, and the barking of dogs. When we reached the spot the fight was already over. The robbers had managed to escape with part of their prey into their inaccessible retreats in the mountains, but the greater portion of the booty had been recaptured. A group of dismounted men was gathered about a form lying prostrate on a ledge of rock. It was Tzang, the leader of the troop. Eager, as usual, to be first in the fray, he had spurred on in front, and had been struck on the chest with a poisoned arrow by one of the retreating freebooters. Dr. Roland drew near, and so skilfully did he dress and cauterize the wound, that after an hour or two's rest the patient was able to resume his seat in the saddle.

During this halt we made amends for our long fast by doing justice to the strange fare spread before us,—roast yak beef, a huge bowl of *tsamba*, and "buttered tea." The last dish caused us a wry face or two, for it was against all our prejudices to see boiling tea beaten

up in a churn, with rancid butter instead of cream, and
salt in place of sugar. The tsamba is oat or barley meal
porridge with great lumps of butter in it; and we soon
learned to relish this strong dish, which was our main
article of diet during our stay in Thibet. When the
march was continued we were mounted on hardy mules,
selected from the herd recovered from the Lu-tze freebooters; and what was to us of nearly as much im-
portance, we were clad in the rude but warm sheep-skin
garments in which the natives can face the rigorous cold
of this high region.

Nothing of unusual interest occurred until, in the
evening, we reached the banks of the Salwen river. We
had to pass over some dangerous bits of road; but
precipices and abysses are as familiar things in this
country as hedgerows are in England, and we left the
matter to our mules, who chose their footing with
unerring instinct. It was, nevertheless, a welcome sight
to us when the deep, green river-valley opened its arms,
as if inviting us to rest and shelter after so long a
sojourn amid inhospitable rocks. The banks at this
point sank down to the level of the stream with a slope
that seemed gentle after what we had lately been
accustomed to, and they were covered with fine trees,
the vivid greenness of whose leaves was in delicious
contrast to the black cliffs around. Below, a beautiful
sward, scattered over with clumps of wood, spread on

each side of a smooth current flowing between rocky islets. Everything spoke of smiling peace and kindly warmth, and a thin yellowish vapour that floated over the water gave a softer charm to the scene.

To our surprise, instead of descending to the bottom of the valley, we halted on the bleak mountain-side, and preparations were made for camping.

"What do these stupid fellows mean by staying up here in the cold, when we might be so snug down in that delightful valley?" asked downright Tom of the doctor. "I see plainly apples and peaches hanging in the trees, waiting to be plucked; and there must be trout lurking in these deep pools, which Han could make into a stew fit for a king, and beat their tea-gruel and buttered porridge all to sticks."

"Content yourself with porridge for to-night, Tom, and be thankful," replied our chief. "You would have been very glad of it last night, when you were looking on with such hungry looks while the bear-steaks were getting brown. I would not advise you to pluck the apples in that paradise; and you may be sure that our guides know quite well what they are about. That deceitful, smiling valley of the Salwen has been of evil omen, since long before Marco Polo wrote that 'any stranger would die for certain' who attempted to cross it."

"How is that, sir?" asked I, while Hannibal looked from the doctor to the river and back in dumb horror.

"Malaria is the name of the demon that haunts it," was the reply. "You can see the sickly mist hanging over it just now. If you went down there, and waited long enough to cast a line, you would be more certain to bring away with you fever and ague than trout. Come away, boys; there will be no fry to-night. Both fish and frying-pan are beyond your reach, and here is a smoking dish of tsamba coming."

"And does nobody live on the river?" we asked, for the mysterious stream excited our curiosity.

"I believe that some of the tribes sow rice in the valley," said Dr. Roland. "They fling in the seed with fearful haste, and snatch their harvest at the risk of their lives. Gold-seekers have also gone down the stream, in search of the yellow metal. There is gold in the sands of all these rivers, and it is regularly worked on the Yangtze and the Mekong; but it is said to be peculiarly plentiful on the Salwen. The treasure-hunters have never returned to tell whether the story was true or not. They have died of the fever, or have been swept down by the wild waves of the Lu-kiang, as the Salwen is named up here. Some of the tribes call it the 'Valley of the Shadow,' because it mostly runs through gloomy chasms, with the cliffs nearly knocking their brows together overhead; and you see that it has two claims to the title."

"And is it the same all the way down"

"Not exactly all the way; for at its mouth—some eight hundred miles from this—you would find your- selves among British shipping and the comfortable bungalows of our countrymen at Moulmein and Martaban. But I daresay there is no stream in the world that has so confined a basin, considering its great length."

"It must be like old Euclid's definition of a line— length without breadth," said Tom.

"But how is dat ribber to be got ober, sar?" was the more practical remark of Hannibal. "Did Massa Polo tell you how him get 'cross, and come back again all 'live?"

"We will see to-morrow morning," replied the doctor, and we could get no further explanation from him that evening.

At daybreak we followed the range bordering the river, and soon came upon the water boiling and roaring far beneath us between steep walls scarcely a stone-throw apart. Gradually the opposing cliffs approached nearer, and we came to a stop at a spot where it seemed impossible to advance a hundred yards further. Our Thibetan guards now prepared to leave us and return home. Their fierce looks and rough boisterous manners had alarmed us at first, but we had found them not unkindly. Their captain, Tzang, took a quite affectionate farewell of the doctor, whom he credited, and I daresay rightly, with having saved his life. He insisted, in token of his gratitude, on pressing upon us, as a present, the animals on which we were riding. Our chief would not hear of this, but at last the matter was adjusted by Tzang accepting in turn a handsome gold chain which the doctor removed from his watch. A few rupees— "wandering rajahs," as they are called up here—were distributed among the followers, and were received with noisy shouts of delight. Tom and I could not help thinking, while all this was going on, that it was scarcely an act of friendship to abandon us on the edge of a precipice, and that unless the mules could jump across the gulf that lay in our path, they could hardly be of service to us. We said nothing, however, as the doctor seemed quite satisfied, and advanced confidently towards two slim lines that we now for the first time noticed spanning the abyss, like spiders' threads. One of these lines, which we found, on approaching, to be of wire chain, started from an elevated point on the opposite bank, and sloped down towards our side, while the other rope was higher on the hither bank. To a platform at the extremity of this latter chain the doctor ascended, seated himself on a sort of leathern sling that moved along the rope on a skid, cast himself loose, and in an instant he had skimmed across to the opposite cliff like a bird. Then unfastening the sling, and adjusting it on the other chain, he slipped back to us with equal ease.

After this illustration of the method of using this

curious bridge, we could have no hesitation, and the
mules and baggage of our party, which still included
the Kashgaree traders, were slung one by one upon the
rope, and launched safely across the chasm. I own
that when my turn came to take my seat on the strap
of rough hide on which the precarious passage had to
be made, I did not feel comfortable. Suspended, as
by a thread, over the gulf of darkness, with the plash
and boom of the torrent rising from below, I felt
awe-stricken and almost terrified. For a moment I
became giddy and faint, but in the next I was standing
securely on firm soil. I think we were all relieved
when, waving farewell to our Thibetan friends on the
other side, we turned our backs on that Valley of
Shadows and River of Death.

CHAPTER VII.

YAKS AND LAMAS.

OR the next few stages of the route nothing very wonderful befell us. The track was more frequented, and more care had been taken in its construction. In some places a narrow causeway had been hewn for a considerable distance along the face of the cliffs, and occasionally the road was carried over strong timber beams driven into the rock, and paved with rough boards or slabs. The track still zigzagged as before from the clouds into the bowels of the earth, and back again into the clouds; but its direction, as we were now on the highway to the famous city of Tali, led us more to the southward instead of due east. There were plenty of signs that we were approaching civilization. The tribesmen whom we met glared at us with greedy eyes, as if they would have liked the excitement of rifling our packs and perhaps cutting our throats; but our resolute bearing and our arms probably prevented attack. They were dressed no longer in skins, but in blue and white cotton cloths, which had probably been woven in Manchester. Herds of goats, sheep, and yaks pastured about their huts, and the patches of level ground were waving with ripe barley, oats, and buckwheat, showing that more peaceable pursuits than robbery and kidnapping filled up part at least of their time.

Then as we approached the "divide" between the Salwen and the Mekong, we came at long intervals on Thibetan grazing-farms and hamlets, and were able to study how this secluded folk behave themselves at home. The great two or three story houses, built of rough stones, without mortar, looked like "border keeps" —as they really are. The tall stature, strongly-marked features, and abrupt gestures of the people; the coarse garments of sheep-skin, drawn in at the waist by a belt in which at least one formidable knife was always stuck; the strange nick-nacks of glass, turquoise, and coral which they wore as charms or ornaments; and the big, fierce-looking dogs that slouched at their heels, were all in thorough keeping with the houses. Within the dwellings there were perhaps more dirt, and confusion, and rude curiosity than we liked; but the hearty good-will and hospitality of the people made amends for all. We were regaled with milk, butter, cheese, eggs, and tsamba unlimited; and we could hardly prevail on these mountain shepherds to take anything in payment. A sight of Hannibal's bare arm of ebony placed alongside of our white skins was thought sufficient recompense, and would make a whole company roar with laughter for an hour.

We were warned, however, that it was all very pleasant so long as we were among the common people, but that when we came across the lamas, who cherish a fanatical hatred of our race and creed, we might "look out for squalls." These lamas, as the reader may know, dwell together, sometimes in communities of many thousands, under a vow of celibacy and in perpetual contemplation of the virtues of their great 'master, Buddha. By all accounts, however, they are a sad set of rascals, who live in ease and idleness on the toils of men more ignorant but more honest than themselves, and who have managed by degrees to gather all the power and wealth of the country into their hands. The cunning knaves fear that if foreign commerce found its way into the country their day would be done, and hence their determination to turn back every stranger from their frontiers.

We had some doubts as to our welcome when we learned that another day's march would bring us to a lamissary highly reputed for the sanctity and learning of its inmates. By rare good fortune, however, we were able to possess ourselves of the means of getting into the good graces of the suspicious monks. We were informed at a Thibetan hamlet that a party of wild yaks, led by a bull of extraordinary size, had been seen lately roving on the slopes of the neighbouring snowy mountain. The doctor resolved to set out in chase, as he had a special wish to study the peculiarities of the wild breed.

Scouts brought in news that the yaks were feeding in a grassy valley in a mass of mountains three or four miles off, and partly in the direction in which we were moving. We learned that at the head of the glen there was a pass over the mountain at some distance above the snow-line; and our plan of action was to send a party of our Thibetan friends, who were easily tempted by the prospect of fresh meat to join the enterprise, to disturb the animals and head them up the valley. They would be almost sure to endeavour to escape over the pass; and here, it was arranged, we should lie in wait to intercept them.

We started at an unearthly hour in the morning, and after a most fatiguing climb reached our posts before the day was far advanced. Here we watched long without any sign of a reward for our trouble. There was no shelter, and in spite of our warm fur coverings we found it terribly chilly work waiting among the snow, more especially as the thick clouds of vapour that rolled about us shut out our view of the world below.

"This is the coldest job we have had yet, and I can't

wonder that even yaks don't like to come up so high," Tom said, rubbing his numbed hands and stamping his feet, while the rest of us also hopped about as if we were executing a new figure in a country dance.

"Hush!" said Hannibal, who had an extremely quick sense of hearing; "t'ink I heah dat big fellow grunt. Ha! ha! you jes' come up heah, will you, and get somefing to grunt for."

We listened, and after a little heard an angry snort like that of a steam-engine, followed by a deep, hoarse, lowing note that might have been mistaken for distant thunder, and by the faint shouts of the beaters. After a brief interval, which, however, seemed to us eager stalkers an age, an immense shaggy head and shoulders rose over the crest of the hill, and a pair of fiery eyes glared around. It was the big bull himself, and a splendid fellow he looked indeed, as he stood for a few seconds petrified with rage and astonishment at the sight of us. The doctor might have got a long shot at him at that moment, but he waited in expectation of the bull coming nearer. My three companions were posted in front of the low pass; while I had taken my station a little to the left, in case the herd should head off in that direction. I had brought with me an old-fashioned rest, borrowed from our Kashgaree fellow-travellers, and on this I now placed the barrel of my rifle, and with a heart thumping with excitement dropped down on one

knee behind it. This curious movement seemed to decide the bull. With a furious roar he charged straight
towards me; while his companions, following his lead,
crested the brow of the hill, and bore down upon us like
a wave of tossing horns, tails, and manes. Our chief
had always strictly charged us against the barbarous
sport of wantonly destroying the wild game for killing's
sake, and in the present case he had only wished to
secure the big male. We were now, however, left with
no choice, and shot after shot resounded in the hills.

As for myself, my whole attention was taken up with
the monster bull, who seemed in a desperate hurry to
make my acquaintance. When he was within fifty
yards I fired. The shot struck him on the shoulder, but
rather low, and he fell bellowing loudly among the snow.
With all the haste I was capable of, I pushed another
cartridge into the breach, and stopped just in time, with
a bullet through the heart, one of the consorts of the
mighty bull as she came pounding down upon me. Meanwhile, the lord of the herd had struggled to his feet, stag-
gered forward some yards, and stood the picture of baffled
rage—his grand front and spreading horns thrown high
in the air, and his eyes blazing with wrath, lashing with
his tail his shaggy sides, and pawing with his hoofs the
snow that was stained with his blood. I drew the
trigger of the second barrel, and with hardly a groan he
fell dead " in his tracks."

My companions had been equally successful in stopping the charge of the younger bull and his mates, who, after each receiving a shot in a vital place, had turned and attempted to escape before getting their final *coup*.

Hardly was this brisk incident over when the beaters appeared at the head of the pass, and great was their rejoicing over our achievement; but for ourselves, I think a feeling of regret at having deprived so many splendid, vigorous creatures of life was almost above our sportsman's triumph.

Having possessed ourselves of the big bull's head, and with as much yak's flesh as we cared to bring away with us, we presented two of the carcasses to our assistants as a recompense for their help, reserving the others as a timely present for the inmates of the lamissary, which could be reached in three hours' ride from the spot where our adventure occurred. On the route we were rejoined by our travelling companions, the Kashgaree merchants, who listened to the details of our hunt with no other response than a solemn " Allah be praised!" at the close. They did not appear to have a large share of the sportsman feeling themselves, and indeed we began to suspect that they were not much of traders either, and to wonder what were really the contents of the strange packages and bales that they carried with them. If I have said little about them hitherto, it has been because I had little to tell. They coldly repelled our attempts to "fraternize" with them, and though they were pleased enough with our companionship so long as we were exposed to attack from the robber tribes, they seemed to feel our presence become more embarrassing with every mile that brought us nearer to the frontier of China. There was certainly something mysterious about their journey and the excellent understanding that existed between them and the Thibetans. But Khodja Akbar Khan, the chief of the party, a grave personage with deeply-marked, sinister-looking features, and a flowing black beard edged with gray, looked the last person in the world to let a secret slip from him, and, judging by a fanatical gleam that now and then shone in his eyes, he would probably have felt more at his ease cutting off the heads of "infidels" like ourselves than in travelling quietly in their company. His two chief associates appeared to be completely under subjection to him, and their half-dozen attendants were as silent as mutes.

Meanwhile it was plain that we were approaching the precincts of the lamissary. We had already seen many signs of the Buddhist faith and worship since we had come into this country. Every other person we met carried a little cylinder, which he kept twirling round, muttering at the same time something half below his breath. At the door of each dwelling stood one and often several larger cylinders of the same type, and every one that

THIBETAN WITH HIS PRAYING-MILL

Page 90.

passed out or in gave the wheel a turn for the benefit of
the household. On the summits of the rocks we observed
other specimens of these prayer-mills—for such they were
—driven by the wind; while at the crossings of streams
we invariably found a little water-wheel revolving with
the current, and enclosing a cylinder written over with the
strange characters that met our eyes wherever we went.
At every pass over the mountains we came upon what
in our own Highlands at home would be called a cairn,
made up of stones left there by faithful devotees of the
Yellow Religion in gratitude for having escaped thus far
the perils of the way, and to propitiate the favour of the
evil spirits of the hills; and on each stone the mystic
letters were inscribed. From the trees by the wayside,
and at the end of long wands hung like fishing-rods
over the streams, fluttered scraps of paper or cloth with
the pious formula repeated upon them, so that a breath
of wind could not blow without wafting to heaven
thousands of prayers from the wayfarers that had passed
over this road. The great sanctity of the monastery
we were about to visit was shown by the lines that
stretched across the ravine which led up to its gates,
and from which dangled innumerable rags of silk or
oiled paper, scribbled over with prayers; and the rocks
on both sides were carved with the never-ending
petition.

We began to meet the inmates of the monastery

walking singly or in twos and threes—tall, strange-looking figures, generally dressed in long gowns of red or green serge, with a yellow scarf across the shoulders, and red boots. Their heads were shaven; and under-neath their black eyebrows they cast disdainful and suspicious glances at us as we passed. Around their necks they wore strings of coral beads like rosaries, and each carried in his hand a little prayer-wheel, which he assiduously twirled while he mumbled his litany. They may have been learned and pious men, but there could be no question that they were deplorably dirty.

"What do these fellows mean by continually mut-tering, 'Niminy-piminy, niminy-piminy,' sir?" asked Tom the querist, turning to our usual source for infor-mation, as we rode up towards the gate of a great pile of blind-looking buildings that now came in sight, and that might have been mistaken for an old feudal "strength" but for the gilded roof rising in the centre, with gables turned up at the corners, like those we had seen in pictures of Chinese pagodas.

"I daresay it sounds more like 'niminy-piminy' than anything else," said Dr. Roland, smiling, "and has about as much meaning to them. They intend to say, 'Om mani pemi hom.'"

"And what does 'Om mani pemi hom' mean, then?"

"It means, 'Oh, the jewel in the lotus.'"

"But," said Tom, looking more puzzled than before,

"I don't see that that makes it much plainer. What is 'the jewel in the lotus'?"

"Nay, you have cornered me now, Tom," said our friend; "whole libraries of books have been written about it, and instead of making it plainer they have only made the mystery more profound. Every syllable has been taken to pieces, and every letter dissected, and the strangest and most contradictory meanings discovered hidden in them. I have no doubt our friends there," pointing to a group that were busily twirling their wheels, "have the whole controversy at their finger-ends, like the prayer itself. It is the universal petition of the votaries of Buddha, and is supposed to be a prayer for that perfection of life which will admit them, after passing through millions of changes, into Nirvana —the state of total unconsciousness which is their sad notion of heaven and future bliss. You may be sure that at any given moment this mystic prayer is being repeated by hundreds of thousands of lips in Buddhist lands."

I am not sure whether the doctor's explanation made us much the wiser, and we were still struggling to comprehend it when we halted at the gate of the lamissary. Notice had been sent of our coming, and the chief lama, with his principal officers, was in waiting for us, most gorgeously dressed in robes of red and yellow, and his head crowned with an immense gilded hat. He was a

weazened-faced old man, whose expression of features
spoke more of cunning and meanness than of benevo-
lence.   I thought I caught a look of intelligence exchanged between him and Khodja Akbar, whose arrival
did not seem to surprise him, and then he turned
towards us with an air that did not bode any good-
will.   On Dr. Roland coming forward, however, and
explaining, as we gathered from his gestures,—for he
spoke in Chinese,—the handsome addition we had provided for the larder of the monastery, the old bonze's
mien underwent a wonderful change, and his features
puckered up into a smile that was meant to be affable.
It is against the strict rules of the order to partake of
the flesh of any animal, for according to the Buddhist
belief it may have harboured the soul of some of their dead
ancestors ; but in these remote mountains the monks do
not keep their vows very strictly.   So our present was
graciously accepted, and a party of men and mules was
hastily despatched to the pass to bring away the carcasses of the yaks before they would be discovered by
the gaunt Thibetan wolves, while we were ushered into
the interior of the lamissary.

  We found ourselves in a spacious courtyard, surrounded on three sides by the living-rooms of the lamas,
with a great temple, highly decorated and gilt, facing
us.   After being shown the lodging which we were to
occupy for the night, we were taken into the temple,

where a huge brazen statue of Buddha was the chief
object, and was surrounded by altars of offering, barbarous musical instruments, and carved dragons and other
fantastic figures. The walls were painted with strange
pictures and devices in glaring colours, while in recesses
were rows of small figures of Buddha in solid gold, rolls
of manuscript, and other treasures. Here, by direction,
we deposited our principal valuables under the care of
the presiding deity. We noticed that even here great
deference was paid by the Buddhist priests to our
Mussulman companions, though what could be the bond
of union between people so widely separated by race
and creed we could not imagine. It could not be love,
for I noticed that on leaving the temple Khodja Akbar
spat on the ground in token of his abhorrence of the
idolaters—though the Buddhists deny that they are idol-
worshippers, and say that the figures in their temples
are only memorials in honour of their great teacher.
The insult was noticed by one of our lama guides, and I
shall not easily forget the look of concentrated hate that
he darted at the offender.

We were afterwards served with an ample meal, in
which the unfailing tsamba and buttered tea formed the
principal dishes; but there was also a variety of small
cakes and confections, in the making of which the monks
showed not a little skill and taste. Our Mussulman
fellow-travellers, as usual, ate apart. They retired early

from the guest-chamber; and as it was slow work exchanging ideas with the monks by means of signs, we were not long in following their example.

The sun was shining brightly in the courtyard when we awakened next morning, the early hour at which we had been up the previous day, and the toils and excitement of the yak hunt, having caused all of us to oversleep our usual hour of rising. To our surprise we found, on making inquiry of the monks, that Khodja Akbar and his company had left before we were up, without taking the trouble of saying good-bye. More than that, the gate of the lamissary was not only closed, but a goodly number of the inmates were gathered about it, as if to bar any attempt to pass through. We could see from the doctor's looks that he was very uneasy and anxious to get off. A plot of some kind was being woven, and we had got entangled in the meshes against our will. Luckily we had resisted the pressing offers of the lamas to take charge of our weapons for us, so that at the worst we were well armed. Dr. Roland asked to see the chief lama, and he came to us with a face that had lost all the forced amiability that it wore yesterday. In fact, without understanding the words he addressed to our chief, we could notice distinctly a tone of insolence in his voice, which grew gradually more marked as the conversation proceeded. We waited anxiously for the upshot, feeling that some dangerous crisis was approach-

ing. The doctor seemed to begin by offering thanks
for the hospitality we had received, and a calm request
that we should now be allowed to bid good-bye to our
hosts. The lama replied in mocking accents, and as the
doctor proceeded to repeat his request more firmly, the
high priest appeared to give an emphatic refusal; while
the men with whom the courtyard was filled drew
nearer in a threatening manner as they heard words
rising high. We, also, while hiding our anxiety as much
as we could, began to get our weapons ready; for we
suspected that though the shedding of blood was for-
bidden to the brotherhood, they were capable of finding
means of making away with troublesome visitors that
would satisfy their consciences on that score.

Dr. Roland appeared to make up his mind that it
was time to act with energy. Drawing his revolver—
a six-chambered one—from his belt, he glanced round
the enclosure until his eye fell on an immense gong that
hung near the convent gate. The sight of it probably
reminded him of the capital practice that he had made
at Hannibal's saucepan, and taking aim at it as at a
target, he fired five shots in quick succession, drilling as
many holes through the sounding brass in a way that
must have sadly marred its after performances. Then,
while we brought our rifles to our shoulders, he turned
on the mob of lamas that had been hurrying up from
all sides, but who now fled helter-skelter, tripping over

each other and on the hems of their long gowns in their
haste to get out of the way of the terrible little weapon.
The chief lama alone held his ground, but his yellow,
wrinkled face was so convulsed with fear and surprise
that it was quite comical to see. He had some notion
of the power of the gun,—indeed, an old-fashioned
flintlock is one of the regular arms of the Thibetan
soldier,—but this marvellous article, with the magical
property of firing without needing to be loaded,
was new to him, and he evidently believed that the
doctor held in his hand the lives of himself and all his
convent. When, therefore, he heard the request to bring
out our mules and to throw open the gate repeated in
stern tones, with the revolver pointed at his head, he
sulkily gave the necessary command to his underlings,
who hastened to obey the order, plainly more anxious
now to see us beyond their walls than they had been a
little before to retain us.

In a minute or two we were again mounted on our
long-eared but sagacious steeds, retreating in triumph
with our baggage, which had not escaped some pillaging,
though we did not care just then to examine narrowly
the extent, and pursued at a safe distance by yells,
curses, and stones from our hospitable entertainers of
the previous evening.

CHAPTER VIII.

ASTRAY IN THE MOUNTAINS.

FOR several hours we rode on with scarcely any other purpose in view than to put as wide a distance as possible between us and our late hosts. Several roads, or rather bridle-tracks, led away in different directions from the lamissary. We chose the one that the doctor's pocket-compass told us agreed the most closely with the line we wished to follow—namely, towards the south-east. I cannot, of course, tell whether the others were as rough and steep, but if they were, I do not believe that the lamas can much enjoy riding exercise. A path more bare, desolate, and savage as to surroundings, or more narrow, slippery, and rugged under foot, we had not yet traversed. The sun glared strongly upon us as we crossed a patch of open country, or scrambled and slipped along a broken mountain-side; while down in the deep gorges into which we plunged ever and anon, we had difficulty in making out the path. Still, we hastened on with all the speed our nags

were capable of, occasionally discussing eagerly the exciting scene in which we had just taken part, and the
motives that could have prompted the lamas to keep us
prisoners, but more often silent; for the roughness of
the track generally compelled us to ride in Indian file,
and to keep all our wits about us. Soon after losing
sight of the lamissary the signs of cultivation and inhabitants disappeared, and for some time we had been
wandering through a region that seemed utterly deserted
by man and beast.

As the sun got low in the heavens the doctor drew
rein in a little green valley, where our hungry animals
at once began to nibble the clover and grass. We were
glad to fling ourselves down on the sward, thoroughly
exhausted with the toils of the day.

"I don't know if we will find any place more snug
than where we are," remarked our leader, "though by
my reckoning we cannot be far from the great Mekong
river. Our friends the lamas will hardly care to come
so far to fetch us back, and I think we may camp here
pretty safe from pursuit."

"Is the country uninhabited, sir, that we have seen
neither men nor houses for the last few hours?" I inquired.

"My notion is that we are in the border-land between
Thibetan and Chinese territory," said the doctor; "and
like other border-lands in barbarous countries, it is not

a quarter to choose for leading a quiet life. I would not have thought you would be so anxious, Bob, to meet with your fellow-men after the little experience you had with the Mishmis and the Lu-tze, not to mention our entertainers of this morning. I am surprised, though, that we have met with no roving banditti, for in this country a troop of these rascals is usually to be found between the settled districts. We must keep our eyes "well skinned" to-night, and not let sleep get the better of us, as it did this morning when we allowed Khodja Akbar and his company to slip away unperceived."

"Have you any idea where he has gone?"

"I should not like to venture a guess about a personage so mysterious; but it is plain that he has not travelled by this road, otherwise, at the speed we have travelled, we would have overtaken him and his company. Between ourselves, I should not be sorry if we have seen the last of them."

"You needn't cook anything for me to-night, Hannibal," said Tom, trying to put the best face on it; "I feel too tired to eat."

"Berry lucky dat is, Massa Tom," replied the negro dryly: "couldn't gib you anyt'ing if you asked for it."

"It was a pity we let those fellows have all these juicy yak-steaks, wasn't it?" pursued Tom, with a mischievous twinkle in his eye.

The question was too much for Hannibal's composure.

Visions of the whole unwashed crowd of lamas feasting on the "roast and boiled" which we had provided for them, while his dear master had not a morsel to eat, rose before him, and he shook his fist fiercely in the direction from whence we had come.

"Don't see any more bears hidin' around, Massa Bob?" he asked, after recovering his good humour.

Involuntarily I glanced along the slope of the hill above, and fancied I caught a glimpse of some dark-looking object suddenly withdrawing from sight behind a mass of rock.   I called the attention of my companions to the spot, and we prepared cautiously to examine it more closely.   This could hardly be a bear, and the idea that occurred to us was that it was some spy watching our movements, whether in the interests of robbers, lamas, or Mussulman traders remained to be seen.   As we ascended the hill, the figure of a man rose from behind the rock and drew near to us, with a singular mixture of eager curiosity and of hesitation in his manner. From his features and other signs, including tattoo-marks on his cheeks, we judged him to belong to the same race of savages whom we had seen scattered by the Thibetans on the other side of the Salwen.   But in the new-comer all the harsh traits were subdued and refined.   He was decently and cleanly clad also, in blue cotton jacket and wide trousers; and altogether there was a certain air of civilization about him which we hardly expected to meet with in such a spot. You may judge if our surprise was diminished when, having approached within a few paces of us, he looked anxiously from face to face, and then rapidly made the sign of the cross, such as is practised in Roman Catholic countries.

The doctor, however, appeared to have a clue to the mystery that puzzled us so greatly, and entered into a conversation with the native, who, by means of signs and a few words of Chinese and French, led our conductor to understand that his dwelling was close at hand, and that he would be glad to conduct us thither. The offer was made with a friendly cordiality that convinced the doctor that it was made in good faith; and in a few minutes we had dragged our stiff limbs into the saddle, and, with the stranger as our guide, were again climbing rocky hills and threading stony passes. In about a quarter of an hour we came upon the upper end of a pretty, winding valley, that, with fine trees shading the small stream flowing through the centre, and a few sheep and goats pasturing on the slopes that rose gently on either side, had a charmingly peaceful and inviting aspect after the rugged and toilsome ways by which we had reached this haven of rest. A neat cottage, surrounded by a few fruit trees, with a little garden in front containing vegetables and even a few flowers, occupied a sheltered nook in the valley. To this the guide led us, and motioned us to dismount; and while our mules began to crop the grass, we seated ourselves under the shady porch of the hut.

Our host disappeared inside, and presently came forth with a huge wooden bowl filled with rich goat's milk, and a pile of crisp barley cakes, which, with a gesture of welcome, he laid before us. Then with a natural feeling of good breeding he withdrew into the background beside his wife, whose shyness would not allow her to come forward, though we could see that in dress and looks she was as unlike her wild unkempt kindred as her husband. It made me almost ashamed, after listening to his declaration a few minutes before that he had no appetite, to see the way in which Tom Wilson "tucked into" the milk and cakes. But the rest of us were not a whit behind him; and the bowl, which had seemed bottomless, was emptied at last. Then after we had rested a little, the master of the hut, whose name, it turned out, was Nga-te, signed to us that it was time to resume the march; and rather wonderingly—for we had counted on passing the night in this pleasant spot— we prepared to follow him down the valley.

On the way he explained to us that a wise and good man of our nation had come among the wild robber tribes of this district, and after years of labour and disappointment, had persuaded them to lay aside their savage habits and their wandering life, and to settle down around him in this valley, where they now dwelt peaceably and pleasantly, tilling the ground and tending their flocks, instead of fighting and plundering. He had taught them beautiful lessons of mutual love and forbearance out of a book; but it was chiefly by his example of self-denying kindness, patience, and gentleness, that they had become devoted to him, as our guide appeared to be, heart and soul. Nga had been searching on the hills for a stray goat when he first noticed us. Something about our appearance gave him the notion that we were of the same race as his pastor, and the longer he watched us he grew the more convinced of the fact, and he was about to steal away and warn the settlement of our coming when we observed him.

Thus discoursing, chiefly by signs, we passed several other cottages, embowered in leaves and with little patches of cultivated ground about them, the occupants of which came to their doors and saluted us with respectful interest, no doubt wondering what manner of people we were and whence we had come.

At a sudden turn in the bed of the valley a lovely scene broke upon us. At our feet was a steep descent, down which the brook at our side bickered in a series of cascades, overhung with masses of beautiful ferns, and by fine trees that were beginning to put on their autumn dress. Below, the hills receded on either side, and the vale opened up to meet a mighty stream, whose turbid current ran like a broad yellow

band across the landscape.   This could be none other
than the famous Mekong, the great river of Cambodia,
whose course, from its unvisited source in the northern
deserts of Thibet to its mouth in the Chinese Sea, probably rivals that of some of the longest rivers on earth.
On this rolling flood, overshadowed on the opposite
shore by lofty pine-clad peaks that dipped their feet in
the water, we gazed for some seconds in awe, though as
yet we little dreamed of the perils and sufferings that
we were to encounter on its bosom.   Then we turned
our eyes on the scene immediately below us.   A score
of houses, mere cabins in size, but neatly thatched and
arranged with some sense of order and taste, were
grouped about a building of rather larger dimensions,
near which was a little chapel surmounted by a cross.
Fruit trees, most of them of kinds which you are familiar
with in the temperate zone, grew thickly about the
dwellings, and trailing plants covered their walls.   So
close were we to them that we could make out the ripe
apples, peaches, and apricots shining among the foliage.
Around the village were fields of ripe or ripening barley,
wheat, and maize; and down near the river were dark
and light tinted plots, which our Assam experience told
us must be "paddy" or rice-fields.   The desolate mountains that surrounded the scene, like the frame of a
picture, only made this green and peaceful little Eden
look more refreshing and inviting to us weary travellers.

CHAPTER IX.

A HAVEN OF REST.

LEAVING our mules in charge of the villagers, who testified as much delight as astonishment at our arrival, we hastened to the house of the missionary, wishing, if possible, to take him by surprise. We were not disappointed in this; for on looking over the trim beech hedge that surrounded his garden, we found him absorbed in the care of his plants, and all unconscious that such guests were at hand. The carefully-propped fruit-trees and the alleys of rhododendron and tall box cast a shade most tempting for people who had been so long exposed to scorching sun and cutting winds. The rustic seat under the veranda, overhung with broad vine leaves and clusters of purple grapes, seemed made for jaded limbs to repose upon. The flowers and ferns, the cool-looking little spring of water in the centre ornamented with pebbles and aquatic plants, the glimpse we got through the open window of books and writing materials, all spoke of a cultivated taste.   But most attractive of all was the worthy pastor himself, as, ignorant of our scrutiny, he bent earnestly over his task of weeding his plants. His rather tall and dignified figure was clad in flowing cotton garments, which in cut were a compromise between the Chinese and European fashions.   He was considerably past the middle age ; and time and care had ploughed some wrinkles on the broad forehead and smoothly-shaven cheeks.   The general expression of the face was one of winning goodness ; but the full dark eyes seemed capable of giving a stern glance, and the kind-looking lips of being compressed with a look of energy and decision.

"Bonjour, M. l'Abbé," said the doctor, in his heartiest tones.

The Abbé Ducrot—for such we learned was the name and ecclesiastical rank of the excellent French missionary —started at hearing so unexpectedly the accents of his native tongue. He looked up quickly, and his eyes meeting the black grinning features of Hannibal, who happened to be directly in his " line of vision," the Dutch hoe which he was using dropped from his hands in his amazement.   I am not sure whether the good man's first idea was not that he was about to be assailed by the Evil One ; and if this notion was dispelled on glancing at the other members of the party, the youthful faces of Tom and myself, and the bronzed features and the ample beard of Dr. Roland, appearing as if by magic just above the level of his garden hedge, were in themselves bewildering enough. A few words from our leader, however, explained how matters stood, and M. Ducrot hastened to us, welcoming us with the warmth of an old friend, and with a charming courtesy of manner, as if we were honoured and long-expected guests.

As the sun had now set, and the nights are cold at this season, we did not linger long outside; and for the same reason, when we had been ushered into the good priest's dwelling, we were glad to gather round the stove, while our host lighted his lamp, and bustled about, with the aid of a native pupil and Hannibal, to lay the resources of his bachelor establishment at our disposal. After our performances at Nga's, we were not able to do so much justice to the good father's fare as it deserved or as he would have liked. We preferred to revel in the luxury of being again surrounded by all the signs of civilized life. Everything looked so home-like that we might almost have been seated in a snug English study. The light shone on well-filled book-shelves ranged round the walls, and a white table-cloth, with knives, forks, and glasses, actually graced the board. Still more surprising was it, perhaps, to see the abbé bring forth a box of prime havannahs, which he smilingly tendered to the doctor. Our host did not smoke himself, but some of his friends at Shanghai had forwarded to him this present, which he would be delighted if his guest could find use for.

This led them on to speak of the European society at Shanghai, which Dr. Roland had visited, and where he had picked up the smattering of Chinese he possessed. Our host, in order to give us lads the benefit of the conversation, good-naturedly spoke in English, which he talked with much fluency. But it did not need this to make us feel as if we were in the presence of a countryman—though, of course, M. Ducrot was not only of different race but of another creed than ours. But away in this remote region, surrounded by savage and hostile peoples, the distinction between Frenchman and Englishman, stanch Protestant and zealous Romanist, so great as that seemed in Europe, was of comparatively little account. Last evening we were in an atmosphere that was loaded with danger and suspicion. Hate and prejudice were barely covered by a thin show of hospitality, and everything was petty, false, and base. To-night we breathed again freely. All was frank, manly, kindly, and honest, and we understood the difference between Christian Europe and benighted Asia.

To our host we were like messengers from another planet, and he eagerly questioned us as to the great public events, the discoveries in science, and the movements in literature and art, since he last had tidings from the outer world: and on all these matters Dr.

Roland was able fully to satisfy him. We recounted our adventures, and presented him with some scraps of old "home" newspapers which we found among our packages. The news in them was three months old, but a year had passed since he had heard from Europe, and he accepted them more eagerly than if they had been crisp bank-notes. In return he told us something of his own experiences in founding this flourishing little colony. It was a history of heroism and devotion, better worth recording than that of our own aimless wanderings, but too long to be inserted here. Even now, when success had so far crowned his efforts, he could not tell when misfortune might come, "like a bolt from the blue," through the hatred of the lamas, the jealousy of the Chinese officials, or the outbreak of civil war, and ruin all his labours.

This led the abbé and our chief to discuss at great length the circumstances of the land and the times; and though the rest of the party did not understand half of what these seniors talked about, we knew that they had found a clue to the mysterious conduct of Khodja Akbar and the people of the monastery. They spoke of China as decrepit and feeble, like some huge giant whom age and disease had made almost helpless. The outbreak of Mohammedan and other rebellions in different parts of the empire had, a few years before, threatened to break up the Flowery Land into discordant fragments, and it had only recovered its unity after a terrible effort. In the province in which we had now arrived—Yunnan—civil war had, raged for nearly a generation; a Mussulman kingdom had been founded and destroyed amid incredible bloodshed. Flourishing cities had been razed to the ground, and by battle, massacre, famine, and pestilence six-sevenths of the population had been swept away. The province, M. Ducrot told us, had no sooner begun to recover from its exhaustion than disturbances were ready to break out again. Reports had come to him of new risings of the Panthays—as the Mussulman rebels were called—in the country beyond the river. The lamas were eager to throw off the yoke of Pekin, and would gladly encourage the insurgents.

Our seniors had no doubt that Khodja Akbar, instead of being a "trader," was none other than a Mohammedan "mullah," or priest, charged with the task of stirring up the smouldering zeal of the followers of the prophet, and probably the bearer of important tidings from some other disaffected portion of the wide dominions of the "Brother of the Sun and Father of the Moon." They were also of opinion that we could not safely carry out our intention of proceeding through China, with the certainty of falling into the clutches of the "white flags" or the "red flags,"—the Imperialists or the Panthays,—or into those of the brigands. Then the question arose, What other route was open to us? The most feasible seemed to be one

that led to Bhamo, on the Upper Irrawady, in the territory
of His Majesty of the Golden Foot. But even in making
for Burmah we would meet "lions on the way," in the
shape of robbers, rebels, and savages, not to mention
lofty mountains and deep rivers.

The doctor suggested the great river, whose hoarse
roar we could hear without, as a means of escape from
our predicament. The abbé shook his head.

"Frenchmen have found it impossible to follow up
that most intractable stream further than the Chinese
frontier," he said, with a touch of national pride. "I
acknowledge the great qualities of your countrymen, M.
le Docteur—their courage, their perseverance, and their
energy—but I cannot admit that they will succeed where
my own compatriots have failed."

"But though Frenchmen were unable to ascend the
river in the rainy season, might not Frenchmen have
succeeded in descending it in the season favourable
for travel? And may not Englishmen?" replied the
doctor, a little amused.

"That is true," said the excellent missionary, smiling;
"but," he added, "you are a weak party, and will be
almost at the mercy of the turbulent and barbarous
tribes that dwell on the river."

"Yes; but we are humble travellers, and not important personages, with grand schemes in their heads
of opening up an unwilling empire to trade, and so we

may escape some of the troublesome notice that greater
folks have met with. At any rate, it will be well to
have the river to fall back upon."

"True, also," said the abbé; and thus closed the first
of many conversations we had on this and kindred subjects, for we had already talked far into the night.

We spent a delightful week at Ping-wan-chin, and
ourselves and our beasts rapidly recruited from our
fatigues. Nothing could exceed the kindness of the
abbé, or the goodwill and helpfulness of the villagers.
We were not idle either. The doctor's notion of rest
included several hours a day of botanizing and geologizing, surveying the hills, gauging the volume of the river,
and similar work. We had even a few mild adventures
in climbing the beetling cliffs on the margin of the
Mekong, and exploring the woods; and one day we had
quite a dangerous "sensation." It happened in this way.
We had been busy all day scrambling over rocks, and
collecting mineral, plant, and animal specimens; and in
the quiet of the afternoon, previous to starting for home,
we rested for half an hour. Dr. Roland had perched
himself on a ledge of rock that overlooked a wide extent
of country; and after having made an outline sketch of
the hills and valleys that the view commanded, was now
thoughtfully smoking one of M. Ducrot's cigars, while
Mandarin, a young Thibetan dog belonging to the abbé,
had fallen asleep at his feet, tired with several hours of

racing and chasing. Not far off I was stretched at full
length on a juniper bush, enjoying its fragrant odour,
so suggestive of " my native heath," and watching the
frantic efforts of a beetle with a burnished-copper back
to climb up a slippery piece of rock. In fact, I fear I
was letting my thoughts bear me away into a kind of
day-dream, when I fancied I heard a pebble fall.
Looking down into the little gully that separated me
from the doctor, to my horror I saw a great mountain
leopard, which had stolen up to within a few yards of
him, and seemed in the act of contracting its muscles to
make a spring. My tongue seemed to be paralyzed with
fear, and before I could utter a word, a little puff of
smoke rose within a few yards of me, accompanied with
the report of a rifle, and the leopard rolled over in the
convulsions of death. It was Tom, who, more careful
than myself, had kept his gun loaded near his hand,
and who had managed just in time to send a bullet
crashing through the great cat's skull.

You should have seen how the doctor and Mandarin
started up, the one from reverie and the other from
sleep, and how the latter barked and growled over the
body, as if he had the whole credit of the performance,
while our chief came up and shook Tom warmly by the
hand. I also grasped the dear fellow's fist hard, with
feelings of deep thankfulness for what he had done, and
with reproachful regret that I also had not been found

on guard and ready for the emergency.   Hannibal said
little, but he looked at Tom in a way that said as plainly
as words that he owed him a good turn, which he would
take the earliest possible chance of repaying.   The
animal Tom had shot was a female, and a search of the
neighbourhood threw light on the extreme boldness she
had shown; for in a recess in the rocks, not many paces
off, we came upon three very young leopard cubs, whose
lives the mother had evidently believed to be in jeo-
pardy.   We brought home the cubs, which were about
the size of half-grown kittens, and prettily marked; and
M. Ducrot was to try the experiment of rearing them.
We have not heard since what was their fate.

The day had now come when we had to bid farewell
to our kind host and the many friends we had made in
the village.   A longer stay with them was not unlikely to
bring the settlement into trouble; and we had not any
time to spare, if we were to make use of the most suitable season for travelling.   The doctor left his scientific
gleanings in charge of the abbé, who in turn loaded us
with everything he imagined would be useful, while his
flock also brought their goodwill offerings.   They gathered
together to assist in packing our mules, and to see us
depart; and, as they had learned from their pastor, they
shouted "Bon voyage!" after us as we rode slowly
away.   Our rest in this happy valley among these
simple, kindly folks had been very grateful to us.   It

was like a half-way house where we had found shelter and a welcome in a tempest, and we felt sad at heart as we prepared to plunge again into the storm. The excellent priest seemed at least as sorry to part with us. He accompanied us some distance beyond the village; and when at last he shook our hands at leaving, I think I saw moisture in his eyes. I am not sure, however, as my own were not very clear at the time.

CHAPTER X.

AMONG THE PIGTAILS.

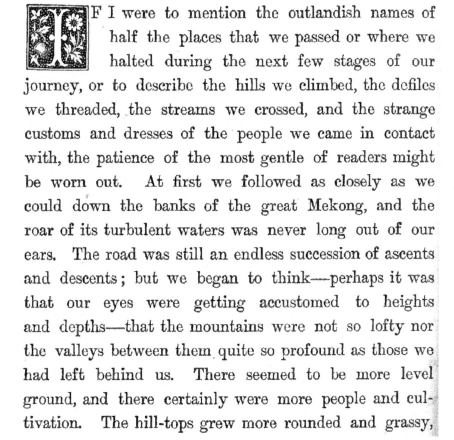F I were to mention the outlandish names of half the places that we passed or where we halted during the next few stages of our journey, or to describe the hills we climbed, the defiles we threaded, the streams we crossed, and the strange customs and dresses of the people we came in contact with, the patience of the most gentle of readers might be worn out. At first we followed as closely as we could down the banks of the great Mekong, and the roar of its turbulent waters was never long out of our ears. The road was still an endless succession of ascents and descents; but we began to think—perhaps it was that our eyes were getting accustomed to heights and depths—that the mountains were not so lofty nor the valleys between them quite so profound as those we had left behind us. There seemed to be more level ground, and there certainly were more people and cultivation. The hill-tops grew more rounded and grassy,

and the slopes of the valleys were less steep, and were
covered with beautiful woods of pine, oak, chestnut, and
other trees.

Sometimes the trees were scattered over a rolling
sward, singly or in clumps, looking like an ornamental
English park, and there were not wanting troops of
deer and coveys of partridges and pheasants to complete
the resemblance. At the bottom of these green and
wooded glens, along the banks of the little tributary
streams, wooden cottages with vegetable gardens, orchards,
and tilled fields became not uncommon.

The doctor pointed out to us how the shaggy yaks
and coarse-wooled sheep that we had seen feeding on
the hills, guarded by rough-coated and loud-tongued
Thibetan shepherds, had disappeared. Their place was
taken by more domesticated-looking animals; and the
people at work in the fields were dressed in light and
loose cotton garments, instead of sheep-skins and furs.
As we advanced southward, gradually descending, rice
and Indian corn superseded the thin barley, oats, and
rye, and plantations of sugar, cotton, and tobacco told
of a warmer climate. The white flowers of the poppy
plant, from which opium is manufactured, blazed in the
plains below us, and mulberry and tea trees showed
where silk or tea culture occupied a busy people. At
length a thicket of bamboos by the side of the river
warned us to keep on the alert for the " big game " of

the jungle—the tiger, the alligator, and the buffalo—as we had fairly returned into tropical climes, after a sojourn in the arctic regions.

The change in the faces and in the manners of the people was even more wonderful. At first, at long intervals, we came on little villages composed of a few huts of stone, huddled together as if to keep each other warm, and not unlike the Thibetan hamlets we had visited. But the natives spoke neither Thibetan nor Chinese, nor any other language that the doctor was acquainted with; and they lived under chiefs who appeared to care nothing for either grand lama or emperor. They were very kindly and hospitable to us, however; and probably it was their picturesque costume,—jaunty little hats perched on their heads, gaily-coloured jackets and embroidered belts, and legs swathed in long rolls of cloth, like Piedmontese peasants,—together with their light shade of complexion and high, well-cut features of almost a European cast, that made us feel more at home among these half-barbarous tribes than we afterwards did among people much more civilized.

When we left these villages, generally loaded with presents from chiefs and people in exchange for the small trinkets we were able to offer them, we found we had bidden farewell to simplicity and homeliness. The paths we now struck upon were still rough and dangerous, but they were more frequented, and great labour and cost had been expended upon them. Tunnels were scooped along the sides of the gorges, and the road, laid with great blocks of stone, was supported for many hundreds of yards over the abysses by great beams. Bridges of stone arched the torrents; and by-and-by we came to a really important work of engineering,—a suspension bridge, hung on heavy iron chains, and crossing, in one span of two hundred feet, the chasm of the Mekong. As there was no longer a track for us along the right bank of the river, we crossed this structure, leading our mules by the bridles, and holding on firmly by the handrails; for the gusts that blew down the gorge made the bridge swing most ominously, and threatened to hurl us over into the muddy current that boiled a hundred feet below us.

Leaving the river, our road then carried us into districts that became gradually more civilized, and yet, to Tom and me at least, more unfamiliar. There could no longer be a doubt that we were fairly within the strange world of China. If we had been suddenly whisked away into another planet, or if a magician had, by a wave of his wand, transported us into some enchanted region, we could not have been more confused and puzzled by the sights that met us. The people were so yellow, smooth, and smirking, so shaven and shorn, their little beads of eyes leered at us so cunningly, and their pigtails hung so funnily from under their

wide-brimmed hats, that we had some ado to keep from
laughing in their faces.   The babies had a look of pre-
ternatural age and wisdom, and the old men looked
like overgrown and wrinkled babies, in petticoats and
slippers.   Instead of the bold, free stride and rude
manners of the mountaineers, our new acquaintances
were soft-footed and insinuating.   The corners of their
eyes were always wrinkling with a joyless grin; and, to
tell the truth, they struck us as more amusing than
attractive.   Most of them seemed miserably poor, but
we occasionally met with a high dame, dressed in richly-
flowered silk and glittering with precious stones, seated
in a sedan-chair, such as our great-great-grandmothers
used, and borne along at a swinging trot on the shoulders
of four almost naked coolies.   We were privileged, once
or twice, to see these ladies dismount, and I do not think
that the humblest village lass at home would have
envied these poor creatures their silks and jewels, if they
had seen them hobble painfully for a few yards on the
mutilated stumps which were all that fashion had left
them for feet.

The ladies and the common people stared at us
strangers with undisguised curiosity, and often openly
burst into shouts of laughter at the comical figures we cut
in their eyes.   They were good-natured enough, however,
and I daresay a British country crowd would not have
behaved better if a party of Celestials had suddenly

dropped among them from the clouds. But occasionally we would meet with an official dignitary in his palanquin, or mounted on a mule, and attended by a score of bearers and attendants; and then we never failed to have a glance of extreme ill-will and suspicion directed at us, and we were stopped till we could explain what we were and whither we were bound. Our leader's tact and patience, and perhaps, also, our bold front, our arms, and the presents we took care to bestow, brought us safely out of what several times looked a serious predicament. Accompanying the mandarin as a guard would be a party of three or four soldiers, dressed in flaming red, armed with bow and arrows, matchlocks, long spears ending in three prongs, and other uncouth weapons, and bearing a red flag, on which sprawled a hideous dragon, all teeth, and claws, and wings, and writhing tail. We noticed that at no great distance from the official party we were almost certain to come upon a group which we had no difficulty in recognizing, by their white turbans and whiskered faces, as "Hui-huis," or Mohammedans, who, notwithstanding the massacres, seemed still to abound in the country; and it certainly occurred to us that they were dogging the steps of the "red flags." They drew aside on the narrow path to let us pass, and glared at us in a way that plainly showed dislike and suspicion; but they did not interfere with us, having, it seemed, more pressing

matters to attend to than a doubtful quarrel with
strangers.

The air, we soon found, was full of alarm, uneasiness,
and wild rumours; and the family parties we had met
were country gentry fleeing to the walled towns for
refuge. Reports came to us that the "Hui-huis" had
again raised the flag of rebellion, and were flocking to
hear a prophet from afar, who had come to preach a
holy war. We were told that if we entered any of the
Chinese towns we would certainly be thrown into prison
on suspicion of being in complicity with the insurgents;
while if we fell into the hands of the rebels, a still
worse fate would befall us.

Thus we kept away as far as we could from the
towns and villages, and tried to approach again the
banks of the Mekong, which we knew must be recrossed
if we were ever to find our way to Burmah and safety.
It was easier to travel unobserved through these country
parts than it must have been before fire and sword had
wasted the land. For hours we would march through
ruined fields and gardens overgrown with weeds, and
the wrecks of cottage homes buried among thorns and
nettles, and from which no smoke had risen since the
blazing embers had been quenched with the blood of the
happy families who had once dwelt here. Now and
then we would come to a wooden shanty, recently built,
and a plot of ground reclaimed from the waste. Thriv-

ing crops of rice, grain, and potatoes grew around; the little garden was full of the beans, cabbages, cucumbers, and other vegetables that the Chinese are so skilful in growing; and ducks, hens, geese, and pigs played round the doors, and made as free with the interior of the dwelling as if the owner had been an Irishman. On seeing a mounted and armed party approach, the poor people would come hastily forth and present us, in fear and trembling, with their offerings of curdled cream, cakes, vegetables, a fowl, or a piece of pork, along with the *khata*, or " scarf of felicity,"—a little square of silk or gauze which fashion requires should accompany every gift in these countries. For dessert we were offered the seeds of the sun-flower, and water-melon plants that were growing round every cottage, which the Chinese crack with great dexterity, but which we could make nothing of; also pears of great size and flavour, which we knew better how to dispose of. Our hosts seemed surprised when we insisted on paying for all we got. They appeared to expect that the " foreign devils " would proceed to butcher them in return for their kindness.

The few passengers we now met on the way were equally fearful and suspicious; and a string of coolies, whom we suddenly met in turning a corner of the rocky road, flung down their packs and fled in dismay at the sight of us. Strange was the merchandise and strange the coin in this strange land. For money we found "bricks" of tea, bars of copper, and loaves of salt, stamped and lettered, in circulation. The doctor showed us among their wares packages of drugs manufactured from bones and flies and lizards and what not, which he said were enough to set on end the hair of every chemist in Europe. He particularly pointed out a collection of caterpillars, each possessing what seemed to be a long projecting snout, which was in reality, he told us, a kind of fungus; and for this repulsive medicine the Chinese were eager to give many times its weight in gold, believing it to be a sovereign remedy for every disease. We were puzzled by finding whole bales of eggs about the size of a pea, which our chief explained were the spawn of the curious wax insect, which are every year conveyed from Yunnan to the provinces farther north and placed on trees, where, on reaching their larva stage, they deposit a wax which is one of the most important articles of commerce in the country.

One evening we had halted for the night at a roadside inn; not one of the "fine hostelries" which Marco Polo describes as having found in this quarter in his day, but a humble and very dingy and dirty place, where the landlord had nothing better to set before us than a mess of rice and a "ham," which, on examination, turned out to be the leg of a dog, and was therefore removed untouched. The doctor plied his pair of "chopsticks" with great skill on his own portion of rice, and looked on smilingly while we vainly strove to lift up a few particles from the plate to the mouth.

"Confound these people and their ways of eating!" growled Tom, eying the dish hungrily. "If I had a spoon now——"

"I think I have had enough," said I, pushing away my plate. I could not get the "dog-ham" out of my head, and felt rather squeamish. "I think, sir, on the whole, I would rather swallow Chinese medicine than Chinese food."

"Don't you think that for folks that will by-and-by be setting up for great travellers you are rather too particular?" said the doctor. "If we are to be long in China, though I hope we won't——"

"Amen!" said Tom and I in a breath.

"You will have to make your minds up to get over many of the little prejudices you have brought from Europe. What would you say, now, to fried rat, or a stew of black cat flesh, which you will find at the best tables here?"

"Ugh! ugh!" we cried, while Hannibal got up and walked about uneasily, with his eyes rolling in his head.

"A dish of black cats' eyes is considered a great delicacy, but I fear that would be beyond our means."

"Ah! please don't, Massa Doctah!" pleaded Hannibal, in a lamentable voice.

"Birds'-nest soup, now," said Dr. Roland, paying no heed to the appeal, "or tipsy shrimps—"

"What are they?" interrupted Tom. "That sounds rather jolly."

"Live shrimps, made tipsy with wine. When they gambol and hop on the dish, you catch them in the air between the chopsticks, and convey them to your mouth."

"I am sure I should never get tipsy on tipsy shrimps," said Tom, shaking his head.

"I was about to say," proceeded the doctor, "that these are luxuries only to be got on the sea-coast; and for a glimpse of the salt water, I daresay, we would be glad to make a meal of these jolly shrimps."

"I believe I would even swallow a whole black cat for that sight," said Tom. "But when are we to see it; what are our prospects now, sir?"

The doctor's voice lost some of the cheerfulness it always had when he was speaking to us, as he replied, "You know what the landlord told me a little ago. The Mekong is just beyond the nearest range of hills, but beyond the river the country is in the possession of the rebels and the banditti. They hold all the regular roads, and a party of traders who attempted to steal through has come to grief. I am afraid that it is only too true, and that our retreat is cut off on both sides—towards the coast, and towards Burmah."

"What must we do, then, sir?" I asked.

" Move on hopefully with the river as we are going, and look out for some way of escape from this distracted empire into the savage countries to the south. If we could only hear of a guide ! I am sure there are routes we could traverse if we but find some one to lead us."

" How can these people be so mad and wicked as to begin fighting again, when the whole land is still full of the misery and ruin of the last war !" I exclaimed.

" Ay, my boy, that is a more reasonable remark than your objection to Chinese food," said the doctor rather sadly ; "but I fear that it applies to more people than to Chinese."

While we were speaking, we heard a hum and a shuffling of feet without; and the landlord opened the door and looked in, with a gesture of apology. What he told the doctor was to the effect that the only survivor of the trading party, whose disaster at the hands of the rebels we had heard of, had been brought to his house, and was now lying downstairs in a dying state. The unlucky fellow, the landlord informed us, was not a Chinaman, but a barbarian—a Burmese Shan. At this news we pricked up our ears, for it was through the Shan country, tributary to Burmah, that we hoped to find a route, and the region was practically unexplored. He had escaped almost by miracle from the knives of the rebels, and, in spite of his wounds, had swum across the river. He seemed now in the last gasp, but he had been brought hither in the expectation that the foreign necromancer would heal him by his magic. On the strength of some simple remedies which the doctor had applied with success, his fame as a physician, or, what means the same thing in China, a sorcerer, had spread abroad, and already he had had brought to him patients wanting a leg or an arm, for the purpose of having the missing limbs restored.

We found the new patient lying in the courtyard, surrounded by a gaping crowd, whom the doctor at once sent about their business. The wounded man had several ugly slashes about his body, none of them of a fatal character, but he was in the last stage of weakness from loss of blood. The doctor carefully bound up his wounds, and took the other measures in his power to give him relief; and he was soon rewarded by the poor fellow opening his eyes and casting on him a grateful look. He was under the middle size, but of a firmly knit and wiry frame, apparently capable of enduring great fatigue. His complexion was a coppery brown, several degrees darker than the colour of the Chinese; his features were more regular and agreeable, according to our taste, and their expression was more open and manly. His name was Yung-wan. The doctor determined that he would stand by him, not only from motives of humanity, but also in the hope that he would turn out to be the guide for whom he had sighed.

CHAPTER XI.

PERILS BY LAND.

YUNG-WAN rallied rapidly under the doctor's care, and in a few days he was able to sit in the saddle. He showed so much attachment to his kind benefactor as almost to arouse the jealousy of Hannibal, whose chosen duty of anticipating all our chief's wants he began to invade. When we were again prepared for a start, therefore, and had explained to Yung the line we proposed to follow, and asked him for his services as guide, we expected a ready consent. A little to our surprise, the Shan hesitated. Some idea we could not fathom seemed to strike him, and he cast a suspicious glance at us, and even made a step or two towards the door. Then another impulse seized him, for he returned and heartily promised to accompany us, telling us that he knew the routes well, and that they would lead us past his own home.

For some days we travelled parallel with the river,

with little of incident to mark our journey. The hills of red sandstone were well clothed with oaks, chestnuts, and other familiar trees, with here and there a stray plant from the tropics. The wooden houses were painted with strange devices of "squirming" dragons and gay-coloured birds; while within the threshold was a little altar, where the family burned "joss-sticks" or squills of aromatic paper to the memory of their ancestors. The people were inquisitive, but not evil-disposed, and seemed all made after one pattern, like their quaint little gardens, and their fields divided like a chess-board. Now and then we caught a glimpse of the distant smoke of a town, or of the red tunics of a body of troops, but to both we gave a wide berth. White watch-towers and many-storied pagodas were perched on the heights, but these also we came not near. . Where we got a peep of the river, it ran in a swift current between great walls of rock that were often perpendicular, and many canoes paddled by nearly naked figures plied upon it. At night fires were lighted on board, and the fishermen might be seen spearing the fish that crowded round the boats attracted by the gleam.

As we travelled, Yung-wan described to us in detail the terrible fate that befell his late companions. The object of their journey he could not or would not explain; but there could be no doubt——for our guide had seen it with his own eyes——that they had been

murdered in cold blood by the rebels, who had evidently
got notice of their movements, and had laid an ambuscade. The leader of the "white flags" Yung-wan
depicted, by a few graphic gestures, as a black-browed,
black-bearded personage, with piercing, restless eyes, and
wearing a huge white turban. We glanced at each
other, for the portrait recalled our old acquaintance
Khodja Akbar, who appeared fated to be the evil genius
of our journey.

Our guide at length decided that we were sufficiently
far from the seat of danger to risk crossing the Mekong,
which here, for once, had a broad surface and flowed in a
smooth deep current. It was tedious work guiding the
mules down the steep, slippery bank to the river margin,
and having them punted and rowed across one by one
in a small barge that served as a ferry-boat. On the
other shore, also, the hills rose steeply to a height of
several hundred feet, and the slope was covered with
great boulders and projecting masses of rock, overgrown
with thorns, brambles, creepers, and stunted forest trees
clinging to every ledge and cleft. Near the summit
was a level cleared space, which we marked out from
below as a suitable resting-place for the night, and
leading up to it from narrow landing-places on the
water-side we could trace two rough tracks through the
mass of jungle and rock.

The path starting from the platform which was the

lower down the stream of the two, seemed to be the
more open; but our boatman landed us at the bottom of
the other, explaining that it was the only one practicable
for saddle animals. If this were the case, we could
only wonder what the lower track could possibly be
like, for a more detestable bit of road we had never yet
met. We had to dismount and, leading our mules by
the bridles, climb and struggle through thickets full
of great barbed thorns and matted creepers, and over
polished and slippery boulders and ragged tree-roots,
now and then plunging into a mud-hole, or falling prone
and sending a cannonade of big stones bounding down
the slope, to the danger of the heads and limbs of our
companions behind. The sweat was pouring from my
brow, and my energies were all directed to keeping my
footing and helping my poor mule over a rock, when,
without any warning, I suddenly found myself pinioned
by a pair of strong arms, and saw the gleam of an immense knife within a foot of my throat. There was a
brief struggle around me—a scuffling of feet, a clash of
weapons, and the discharge of a shot or two—while I
vainly strove to set myself free; but before I could
well comprehend that we had fallen into an ambuscade,
the whole party had been overpowered, and were prisoners in the hands of an enemy who outnumbered us
by ten to one. Where our captors had sprung from I
could hardly imagine, for we had carefully surveyed the

ground before beginning the ascent, and had seen no trace of a human being. The ferrymen were plainly in the plot; and indeed we had reason to believe that there had been spies watching our least movement since we had entered Yunnan. The trap, however, did not catch all the victims; for in the midst of the confusion I got a glimpse of the lithe form of Yung-wan slipping from the grasp of his assailants, and creeping like a serpent into the jungle.

We were hurried unceremoniously up the rest of the ascent. Our rifles had been dragged from us, but the doctor still held his in his hand, and looked so threateningly that none of the bandits ventured to dispute its possession. We took courage from his calm and determined bearing; and as resistance would have been worse than useless, we submitted to the guidance of our captors with the best grace we could muster.

When we reached the cleared space above, it was no longer empty and bare as we had seen it from the river. A group of perhaps twenty scowling cut-throats, armed to the teeth, was collected round a white standard stuck in the ground, and in front of them stood a black-bearded man, with eyes that fairly flashed with hate and triumph from under his dark brows and enormous white turban. Our presentiment had come true. It was Akbar himself! For some unknown reason—unless it were the mere blind prejudice of race and creed—

he bore a fierce grudge against us, and had become the
" rock ahead" of all our plans.   He greeted us with a
mocking, contemptuous smile, but made no other sign of
recognition. . His followers fingered their knives, and
looked at him as if eagerly awaiting a signal for massacre.   The doctor glanced round coolly, as if taking a
survey of the whole situation, and then, still holding his
gun, took a step or two nearer to our arch foe.   My
eyes had followed those of our chief, and looking below,
I observed, though no one else seemed to notice it, the
boat leaving the spot where we landed, and drifting, as
if by its own will, down-stream.   The boatmen had
abandoned their post, and were hurrying up-hill to share
in the plunder; and the idea flashed across my mind
that Yung-wan had something to do with the movement
of the craft.

My thoughts were recalled by the voice of the doctor
addressing Khodja Akbar in firm, temperate tones,
reminding him, as I understood from the gestures, of
the good offices we had paid to him, and asking for an
explanation of his violent and lawless treatment of us.
The only reply vouchsafed was a few muttered words,
and a sign to one of. his followers to take the doctor's
gun away from him.   Our leader turned upon the man
so fiercely, that the latter fell back a step or two; and
then Khodja himself, with an ejaculation of rage, laid his
hand on the barrel.   It was high time to act.   The rebel

soldiers and brigands—for there seemed a mixture of both—had their swords drawn, and several had lighted the fuses of their matchlocks. The insurgent chief had not counted on one weapon which an Englishman always carries about with him. The doctor, retaining his hold of his rifle with his left hand, with his right "let out" with all his strength in the face of the insolent miscreant, who dropped to the ground as if he had been shot.

"Run for the boat!" he shouted to us. "Take the right hand path!"

I had expected this order, and tripping up the big rascal who had first seized me and still retained his hold, I started to run down-hill by the track that led to the lower landing-place. Tom and Hannibal were not so well prepared. They seemed to take the doctor's action as the signal for a general onslaught, and wrestling themselves free, they "pitched into" the nearest of the enemy in the most vigorous style. Perhaps, after all, this was the happiest course that could have been taken; for the Chinamen fell back, astonished at this lesson in fisticuffs, and before they had quite recovered, Dr. Roland seized the victorious warriors by the collars, and by main force wheeled them round and launched them in the direction he wished them to go, following in hot haste in their steps. Meanwhile, in beginning my flight, my eye fastened on the doctor's precious note and sketch book, every leaf of which I knew he valued at a "king's ransom," lying in the grass, where it had been unheedingly dropped. The impulse seized me to swerve aside and to pick it up. Lucky it was I did so ; for at the instant I stooped, a three-pronged spear hurtled over my head, and my nearest pursuer, who had made a prize of my rifle, stumbled over me and came crashing to the ground. Seizing the gun, I continued my flight, being now last in the race. Down we went pell-mell, leaping over rock and stump, and tearing " like mad " through briers and lianas, with a yelling crew at our heels, and a shot occasionally whizzing past us. Our late practice in hill-climbing stood us in good stead, but how we ever reached the bottom without broken necks or limbs, I could never understand. In the boat, with a broad grin on his face, stood Yung-wan the guide, to the unutterable astonishment of Tom and Hannibal. We spent no time in explanations, but, leaping into the boat, pushed well out into the current before our pursuers reached the shore. We had lost baggage and baggage animals, and part of our ordnance, but had saved sweet life and liberty, and bore away no scratch from the battle beyond what the thorns had inflicted.

CHAPTER XII.

PERILS BY WATER.

AT first, however, our safety did not seem so well assured. We were followed along the slopes and brow of the hill by the whole "rebel army," and shots, some of them, no doubt, from our own captured guns, fell about us in the water. We lay down flat in the boat, so as not to afford a target, and thus escaped injury, though two of the bullets actually struck the craft and caused ugly leaks. After a little the firing ceased. The boat seemed to slide with the stream with a new impetus, and a hoarse roaring that we had heard for some time became louder. The enemy on shore sent up a triumphant shout, and I raised myself and looked around. We had drifted for more than a mile from the scene of the late encounter, and the river was swinging round a curve, and entering one of those gorges with sheer walls of rock of which we had already seen too much.

There was only an hour of daylight left as we shot

into this dark portal. The current was already turbid
and strong, and deeply coloured with the red clay from
the hills. The tall cliffs threw their shadows on the
water, which looked like a rolling torrent of blood. Way
of escape there was none, for the rocks on either side rose
so smoothly and perpendicularly that a squirrel could not
have climbed to the top. Ahead was a broad line of
white, and the roar of the tumbling flood became so loud,
that we had to shout in order to make our voices heard
by each other. For aught we knew, it might be a
cataract with a sheer plunge of a hundred feet to which
we were hastening helplessly; but Yung-wan, who
seemed perfectly aware of what lay ahead, signified to
us that these were only "rapids," and we gathered more
confidence. We had pulled well into the centre of the
stream, and now saw before us a dark opening in the
line of foaming and tossing water; and for this we
struggled literally for dear life. In a second or two, and
before we could properly collect our thoughts, we were
on the edge of it—an inclined plane of water, glassy with
exceeding swiftness, while on either side the angry
stream poured over a ledge of rocks seven or eight feet
in height. I remember the idea curiously occurring to
me, as we sped down the smooth slope with the swiftness
of an arrow, that it was like the bit of unbroken water
that one often sees between the snowy tops of a line
of breakers. Next moment I was holding on to the side

of the boat with all my might, as it heaved and rocked and spun round and shipped quantities of water in the boiling pool below the rapids. With much ado, and mainly by the skilful steering of Yung-wan, we managed to sheer clear of the whirlpools and rocks. And then "again we urged our wild career;" for new rapids, and reefs, and boiling caldrons, and contending currents followed, mile after mile, in uninterrupted succession. The thunder of the falling water was constantly in our ears, and we were wet through with the spray from the rapids. The boat sometimes was quite unmanageable. It polkaed and waltzed, and curvetted like a horse rebelling against a tight bridle, in the eddies, in a way that might have seemed comical from the shore, but to us appeared in quite a different light. Then, as the current caught it, it would bound forward, like a steed with loose rein, until another eddying pool would bring it up.

At last there seemed some little prospect of smoother water. For half a mile we had had no rapids, only a swift current beaded with foam, that churned against its banks, and was broken here and there by ripples from a submerged rock. We were busy bailing out the boat, which was half filled with water, when we became aware that another danger lay in store for us. The walls of the cañon contracted, and the stream, narrowed to half its former breadth, rushed like an enormous mill-race down a steep, confined channel,

interrupted by rocks and cross currents. A glance at
the prospect ahead told us that the boat in its present
condition would certainly capsize if we attempted to
shoot these formidable rapids on board of it. In almost
less time than it occupies to tell of it our measures were
taken, under the directions of the doctor and Yung-wan.
We stripped off our clothes, wrapping in them the guns,
our slender stock of ammunition, and the note-books, for
protection against the wet. Already we had fastened
short lengths of rope to the gunwale of the boat, in
anticipation of an upset. At the head of the rapids, as
the crazy craft began to tilt and rock in the surf, each,
keeping a firm grip on his little cable, slipped over the
side into the wild chafing torrent.

Away we went at "express speed," borne like chips on
the troubled stream, first down into a deep trough, as if
we were about to search the stream to its bed, and then
heaved up on a ridge of water, like a huge wave. The
boat kept a pretty even keel, for we acted on either side
of her like outriggers, and the velocity of our course
seemed to keep our heads well above surface. But once
or twice a sudden swerve of the craft sent me for a
second or two completely under water. As we rose out
of another hollow and crested the last watery ridge, I
caught a momentary glance of a seething mass of foam
below me, and beyond that a wide pool in which eddies
were circling and masses of water were welling up like

great boils, as the river prepared to take a more gentle flow through a more open country. It was the bottom of the rapids and the end of the cañon—safety and deadly peril in conjunction. Instinctively my fingers closed like a vice over the rope, and next instant the light of day was shut out. There was a singing and buzzing in my ears, as the waters closed over my head, and my whole faculties seemed to be concentrated into "holding on."

I could only have been a little time under water, yet it seemed an age, during which I was in desperate conflict for my life with the evil spirits of the Mekong, before I again raised my head above the surface and looked round. The boat, full almost to the gunwale with water, was turning slowly round in the pool below the rapids. The doctor and Hannibal were shouting my name and that of Tom from the other side of the craft, and I was able feebly to respond. The Shan guide, also, I saw near me. But where was Tom, gallant, honest Tom? The rope by which I saw him clinging a few seconds before was hanging limp beside me. Had the cruel flood of the Mekong sucked him down? and was that warm, noble heart already growing cold in its unfathomed abysses? A great lump rose in my throat, and the scene swam round me till I felt as if I could lose my own hold and sink after my dear companion. A shout from trusty old Hannibal recalled me to my senses. He had struck out from the boat, and was making his way by vigorous strokes towards the foot of the falls. Looking in that direction, I thought a dark object showed itself for an instant in an eddy, and again disappeared. Powerful swimmer as he was, it was with great difficulty Hannibal made headway through the surface currents and still stronger undertow. At length he dived. Striving with all our power to prevent the boat from drifting away from the spot, we waited breathlessly, but for a long time in vain. We were giving way to despair, when the black woolly head of Hannibal emerged some distance below us. He seemed to be supporting something, and he gave a signal for help. Before we could reply, Yung-wan had left us, and was making his way through the water like a fish by short rapid strokes. I was barely able to retain my hold; but the doctor cleverly guided the boat toward the group. Tom was unconscious, but, we hoped, alive. The guide had relieved Hannibal of the care of him, for the worthy negro was completely exhausted by his exertions. Fortunately the stream bore us of its own accord behind the shelter of a big rock, and we managed to scramble on shore. Our first care was given, of course, to Tom, and we had the exquisite pleasure, after a few minutes, of seeing him open his eyes, look round on us in a bewildered way, and then, with a faint smile and a gleam of his old fun, ask " which of us had fished him up."

We had barely strength to secure our boat; and then we cast ourselves down on the rocks, supperless, and without troubling ourselves to look for a softer resting-place, humbly thankful that we had all come safe out of such terrible peril. The sun was only setting, and on referring to the doctor's watch we found that only thirty-five minutes had elapsed since we entered the gorge. In that time we calculated that we had run seven or eight miles, and descended nearly a hundred feet.

We questioned the doctor whether he had ever shot so dangerous a passage in his canoeing experiences in the Hudson Bay country. He was not sure but that he had; "but never," he added, pointing to our boat, "in so clumsy a tub as that."

CHAPTER XIII.

SWAMPS, SHANS, AND SAVAGES.

WHEN I awakened next morning I was in a terribly battered and bruised state. I had slept the sleep of exhaustion, and had not felt the sharp corners of the stones digging into my ribs and the "small of my back," or noticed the attentions that the mosquitoes and other insects had paid to my prostrate form, and now I smarted for these hours of oblivion. I rubbed my eyes vigorously and looked about me. It was some time before I could realize where I was, and I had a confused notion, partly arising from a loud booming in my ears, that I had gone to the bottom of the falls and never come up.

One thing at least was clear, we were no longer in China—at least in the China we had seen beyond the rapids. There the country was open, settled, and cultivated. The sights and sounds were sometimes so familiar that one might fancy he was in the midst of an English landscape. Everywhere there were signs of

long occupation, a busy and civilized people, and a
climate that knew the changes of summer and winter.
Now, all at once we were introduced into the heart of
an untrodden wilderness. The hills drew back from the
river, leaving between them and the margin room for a
jungle, marshy in some places and rocky in others, composed of bamboos and other tropical plants, woven into
a dense mass by creepers and by high grass and undergrowth. Some tall trees, mostly palms, rose above the
thicket, and their long plumes showed like standards and
pennons above an army. More open forest began at
the foot of the hills, and stretched up to the summits of
the lower spurs. All was wild, luxuriant, tropical. For
aught we could see, the presence of man had never disturbed this solitude, and certainly there was no path for
him on land, except by cutting a lane through the rank
vegetation. The only movement was that of the coppery-
coloured flood that rolled past, flecked with foam, and
the only sound was the dull roar of the cataract, that
seemed to rise and fall as we listened.

We were not long in discovering that there was
plenty of life about, though it was not visible at first
sight. Our earliest move was to the river brink for a
dip. Hannibal took a fine header from the bank, and
I was watching his dusky body as it moved through the
water, while preparing to follow him, when his face
appeared above the surface, his eyes almost starting

from his head with terror. He climbed with extraordinary alacrity upon one of the rocks that strewed the
margin, just as a long snout emerged from the stream,
and a pair of ugly jaws, armed with formidable teeth,
snapped viciously within a yard of him. It was a
crocodile; and we soon found that the river swarmed
with these hideous reptiles, so that henceforth we were
more cautious in the times and places selected for
bathing.

"No life!" cried the doctor, echoing a remark I had
made a minute or two before. "Take care that there
is not a great deal too much life for your comfort. Just
look at Tom's face and neck. I am sure I could count
the marks of the stings and bites of at least a dozen
different kinds of insects, to say nothing of the leeches
that have been feasting on the parts of his nether limbs
that his tattered trousers don't cover. Shall I classify
them for you, Master Wilson? There's a red pimple on
the bridge of your nose, now. Its size and colour show
that a soldier-ant must have been visiting you in your
dreams—"

"I should like to classify them and dissect them too,"
said Tom, looking round fiercely in search of his tormentors. "The flies and ants and hornets and spiders
and the rest are bad enough, sir, but the leeches are the
most abominable wretches. Why, I have shifted my
place several times, and on each occasion a score of these

little demons have gone for me at once. Here they are, you see," pointing to several small black creatures, the thickness of a stalk of grass, that were making towards him with a curious somersault movement, "actually tumbling like clowns on the sawdust, in their haste to suck me dry."

"They must smell the blood of an Englishman, like Giant Blunderbore," I suggested, picking off an intruder which was making its way into my own boot.

"Talking of Blunderbore," said Tom, "I am glad that we have dropped out from among the Chinese, even though we have fallen among leeches."

"I am not at all sure whether we will not drop into China again as we advance," remarked the doctor "But what has Blunderbore to do with China?"

"I must confess, sir," replied Tom, with a look of penitence, "that I felt like an ogre all the time we were there. It was very wrong, I know, but I had an inclination to send my foot through their houses and kick them all over the place. They were so small and flimsy and toy-like, they seemed only set up, like 'Aunt Sallies,' in order to be knocked down. Then the people, with their queer, shiny, yellow skins! I don't know whether their faces looked more comical when they were young and smooth, or when they were old and creasy. And oh, their funny topsy-turvy ways of doing things; and those ridiculous pigtails!" and here Tom fairly burst into a fit of laughing, in which, I am ashamed to say, we joined him. "Several times the idea struck me to seize a dozen of them by these pig-tails, sling them over my shoulders, and carry them off to my castle, like one of the giants in the story-books. But it was the conceit of these people that took away my breath," continued the young man, amusement giving way to wrath. "Why, they looked at us as if it were we who were the barbarians and the guys. Do you remember that old fright of a mandarin we met the day before yesterday, sir, with the big glass button on his hat, and nails like birds' claws? He stared at you like an owl through his great goggle spectacles, as if he were ever so much wiser and more learned than you."

"So, perhaps, he was," said the doctor severely. "And it would have been worth while having a peep through these Chinese spectacles. It would take down the conceit of all of us, Master Tom. No doubt you look as absurd and frightful in their eyes as they do in yours, and who knows whether they have not as much reason? Do you know what I overheard the mandarin's daughter say, whom you seemed to think a good deal less ridiculous than himself?"

"I don't know," said Tom with some curiosity. "I thought she looked my way."

"She said, 'How like a devil he looks!'"

"That was too bad of her," said Tom in an aggrieved

voice. "I don't know why she should have said that."

"Because their notion of ugliness includes blue eyes set under straight brows, a well-developed nose, and red hair."

"But my hair is not red," argued Tom.

"But that whisker for which you are looking out so anxiously promises to be of that hue. We must not be censorious on other people's tastes and manners. I have no doubt that every look and movement of ours offended the old mandarin's sense of propriety; for he is one of the great literati, and has all the wisdom of the Celestials at the end of those long finger-nails of his. If he had understood English, he would have had something to say to you, Tom, about your use of slang," added the doctor, as a parting shot, and to bring the colloquy to an end; for our frugal breakfast, mostly plucked from the trees growing about us, was now over, and it was time to think of resuming the voyage.

The Mekong had now spread out to a breadth of half a mile, and was a magnificent river, with a strong, deep current. We could hardly believe it was the same stream that we had found contracted between precipices and plunging over rocky ledges just above. We had several times, it is true, to career down rough and broken bits of water, which a day or two ago would have seemed dangerous, but after our late experience we thought this mere child's play. Our boat also was better able to encounter these passages; for we had given it as thorough an overhaul as we could, plugging up the holes and calking the seams with the tough fibres of the leaves of a species of palm, which Yung-wan pointed out to us, and which Dr. Roland was of opinion might form an important new substance for rope manufacture.

Indeed this portion of our journey was that in which we had most leisure and opportunity for studying the natural history of the strange lands we were exploring. Dropping down-stream with the current, which bore us on swiftly, yet not so fast as to prevent our noting the objects of interest on the bank, the doctor was continually on the outlook for new facts in botany and zoology, to store up in his note-books, which gradually swelled out almost to bursting. I need not say that we enthusiastically seconded him in his researches, so that the boat voyage was full of enjoyment and instruction, though it had also its discomforts. The insects that had been so prompt in making their calls on our arrival in this region never left us; but we became inured to their attacks, and we learned from the doctor to extract comfort and information out of miseries. He discoursed of the curious habits and wonderful intelligence of our tormentors,—pointing out to us a huge spider, lurking at the bottom of an ingeniously-constructed trap, closed by a hinged door, that he held half open with his foot, while he enticed his unwary prey within by a sweet fluid with which his den was smeared; or a long train of ants, each bearing a fragment of leaf, and marching in military order, under the direction of their generals, colonels, and captains, who gave orders by a touch of their antennæ to those of lower ranks, while their scouting parties were thrown out in front, in order to give warning of danger. He showed us other varieties of ants that lived by fighting and slave-hunting, compelling their weaker brethren to quarry and build for them, and even to notice the baby-ants and feed the lazy old tyrants of parents; and still other kinds that actually kept "dairy cattle"—little green insects that sucked the juices of the wood and leaves, and who were regularly "milked" and watched by their masters. A hundred things that would have escaped our attention, in the water, among the grass, and on the trees, were pointed out to us by our kind teacher and friend. Little bits of bark, or lichen, or stick turned out, on being examined, to be beetles, or bees, or locusts, or spiders; and crumpled and withered leaves, on being approached, spread gorgeous wings of purple, scarlet, and blue, and sailed away in the shape of butterflies, or disappeared out of view with a spring that betrayed them to be crickets in disguise. Often the doctor made us land, in order that he might possess himself of some new or peculiar orchid or fern, growing, perhaps, far out on some overhanging branch; and no conservatory could have shown a more brilliant show of blossom, fruit, and foliage than our boat sometimes did.

We had to be cautious, however, in our botanizing; for, not to speak of the thorns that stabbed like poniards, and sharp-edged blades that cut like razors, there were scorpions and other venomous creatures lurking among the leaves, and it was difficult to distinguish a serpent coiled round the stem of a tree from the twisting roots and branches of the vines and other creepers. In the river we had plenty of opportunity for studying the water-tortoises and snakes—some of the latter beautifully-marked slimy things—that swam with their heads at the surface with a slippery ease that made the flesh creep. The crocodiles were only too familiar, and we could not afford to waste powder and shot on them; and the lizards we did not mind, even when they were as big as young alligators. It was curious, however, to watch the little "dragon-lizard," as it spread its membraneous flippers like wings, and sprang nimbly from branch to branch in chase of the insects on which it fed. We saw plenty of noisy troops of parrots, macaws, hornbills, pigeons, and other birds of gorgeous colour and harsh voices; and the monkeys were such constant attendants upon us at our halts, and kept up so incessant a chattering, that they soon became a nuisance.

As to the nobler forest animals, we did not see much of them. The doctor shot two fine deer, but we only got a distant sight of a rhinoceros breaking his way through the bamboos in a great hurry to get out of our sight. A buffalo, with a magnificent pair of horns, who was enjoying himself by rolling in a muddy pool, got wind of us as we were stalking him, and we did not think it worth while wasting one of our few remaining cartridges in a long shot. A troop of wild elephants that we came upon might have yielded something to our " bag," but it happened that our larder was full at the time—the river yielded us several varieties of capital fish—and we had no desire to kill these splendid creatures for the mere love of slaughter. On the other hand, we would gladly have put a bullet through any tiger or leopard had they come our way, but they prudently kept out of sight, though I daresay the jungle contained many of these " big cats."

We were not long in discovering that the country was not, as we had at first supposed, uninhabited. At the close of our second day on the river we sighted a little thatched hut, some distance back from the river bank, and set on high piles, apparently to preserve it during the floods, while a small skiff was drawn up on shore. Not knowing what reception we might have, we took care to avoid notice, passing down the stream under shelter of a wooded island, and camping on another rocky island for the night. Next day we came upon more huts, some of them standing solitary on their perches in the marsh, like long-legged herons, while others were drawn together into little villages. The natives were out upon the river in their boats fishing with spear and angle; and after much parleying we came to an understanding, and ventured to pay them a visit. The men were almost entirely naked, but their chests and legs were tattooed in elaborate patterns, and their manner of wearing their hair in a round tuft on the crown of the head, the rest being shaven, was probably considered by them ornamental. The women wore bright-coloured pieces of cloth, and were adorned with a profusion of beads and silver anklets, bracelets, and necklaces. We were soon good friends with these simple wild people of the river, who were very different from the ferocious savages who had hunted us among the mountains. They were timid and slow-minded, and looked at all the marvels we had with us,— our guns, for instance,—with a kind of stupid wonder, contenting themselves with setting them all down as the results of magic. Nothing took their fancy so much as the large nails in the soles of the boots worn by the doctor, and they got the notion that here lay the charm by which we were able to do all the incomprehensible things that we showed them.

One afternoon when our chief had lain down, after

a hard forenoon's work, for a siesta, on the bamboo bench in one of the huts, while we rested under a huge banyan tree close by, Hannibal startled us by jumping up declaring, in a great fright, that he had seen "foah niggahs" steal into the shanty. We thought he must have been dreaming, but hurried with him to the entrance, and there sure enough was a group of natives around the still sleeping doctor, pointing out to each other, with awe and admiration, the rows of nails in the stout shoes, while one stooped down and, with a scared face, ventured to scrape one of the mysterious objects with his nail. A shout from Hannibal caused him and his companions to spring almost to the roof of the hut, and their tufts of hair to stand almost erect with dismay; while the doctor sat up, and rubbing his eyes, asked what it was all about. Hannibal was terribly indignant at the liberty that had been taken with his master's person; but the latter only laughed.

Our naked hosts were not savages in the strict sense of the word, for around their houses were some plots of cultivated ground, and they reared large numbers of poultry. After their lights, too, they were followers of the faith of Buddha; and near each village there was a wretched shed, open on three sides to the winds of heaven, with a patch of reed thatch hanging over it like a ragged umbrella, and this we found was their apology for a "pagoda." Further down the stream we reached structures more worthy of the name, and the surroundings changed again as rapidly as in a transformation scene. Again the landscape became of the "willow pattern." Towers of stone and pagoda roofs glimmered far up the heights among the woods; the lower slopes were laid out in terraces, where sugar, tobacco, cotton, and the poppy plant were grown; and the flat ground beneath was occupied by "paddy fields," divided and watered by innumerable canals and ditches. Little bridges, carved with quaint figures of impossible animals, crossed these streams, and they were lined with willows, poplars, and here and there a wide-spreading banyan, from beneath which the painted walls of cottages peeped, while poultry pecked and pigs grubbed in the courtyard around. The rice-harvest was now ripe, and the fields were full of busy, dapper little figures, all shaven and pig-tailed, gathering in the yellow grain, and heaping the straw into stacks like our hayricks at home. It actually seemed as if the doctor's prophecy had come true, and that we were slipping back into China.

These busy harvesters, however, were not Chinese, though they had borrowed most of their civilization from the Flowery Land, and we were now where the word of the imperial ruler of Pekin had little weight. Some tame elephants that moved to and fro, carrying large burdens, and groups of hump-backed cattle, re-

minded one of India rather than China. Strange-
looking pyramids of stone, ending in a spire, that recalled pictures we had seen of Burmese and Siamese
buildings, rose near the villages. We were actually in
a district of the secluded Shan State of Kiang-mai,
which is claimed by the King of Burmah as part of his
dominions, though his title is disputed by the Emperor
of China, while the natives are generally able to
maintain their independence against both these poten-
tates.

This information we got from Yung-wan, who was
quite at home among his countrymen; and I believe
that it was through his influence that we were able to
come and go unmolested, and received so much kindness.
We soon saw a hundred points of distinction between
them and the Chinese. They were gayer in manner
and more gaudy in taste; and, apart from the differences
of feature and language, we could at once tell a Chinaman among a group of marketing people by his plain
dark-blue or white raiment, contrasted with the gorgeous
hues of crimson, purple, and green worn by the Shan
ladies and gentlemen. As for the "phoonghees," or
priests, their flame-coloured robes almost blinded one
with their splendour. The Shans were more bold and
open in speech, and, we thought, walked with a freer and
more manly gait. They seemed also more truthful,
and more cleanly in their persons and houses, than the

Celestials, which is not saying much; and as hospitable
and good-natured, which is saying a great deal.

It may be that this favourable impression arose simply
from our efforts to understand and sympathize with the
people; for the doctor had made us thoroughly ashamed
of our prejudices, and Tom admitted that he had not
felt in the least degree a return of his " ogrish " humour.

However that may be, we had certainly much reason
to be grateful for the kindness we received at a time
when we stood sorely in need of attention; for each of
us had a touch of fever, as a result of our sojourn in
the marshes, and we were detained for over a week in
one of the largest of the Shan villages, which from its
size might almost have been called a town. We chafed
at the delay, to the great surprise of our entertainers,
who had no idea of the value of time, and, like other
Orientals, were never in a hurry. But the interval was
not ill spent, for we had an opportunity of studying
the curious collection of people of different races that
gathered every third day to market, and which embraced
not only many tribes of Shans, but Chinese traders in
copper, salt, and precious stones; sleepy-eyed Laotians,
bringing fruits and spices from the regions further down
the river; Burmese pedlers, with Manchester prints and
Birmingham hardware for sale; natives of Siam and
Anam, and savages in all stages of nakedness and every
pattern of tattoo.

From this point, Yung-wan informed us, there was a route that would bring us to Mandalay, or to the British possessions on the Lower Irrawady. We had engaged a crew of canoemen to carry us up a tributary which here falls into the Mekong. It was impossible, however, we found, to start until we had taken part in the great annual festival in celebration of the ingathering of the rice-harvest. I will not venture to describe the barbaric scene,—how the flags flaunted, and the gongs crashed, and the trumpets blared; how the adults feasted and revelled, and the young people danced and scattered flowers, and the phoonghees scattered incense and walked in procession, followed by the heavy-footed elephants bearing the emblems of the bounteous harvest. But I will always have a picture in my mind of the broad, magnificent river, as we saw it between the stems of bamboos and the leaves of palms and other tropical plants, illuminated by the torches of hundreds of boats that passed backwards and forwards on its waters, while the songs of the rowers reached our ears in a wild and weird chorus. It was the last glimpse we had of the mighty Mekong. Next morning we started westward, before the mists had risen from its surface, on the last stage of our weary wanderings, which would land us again, we hoped, among our dear countrymen.

CHAPTER XIV.

A CANOE VOYAGE UP-STREAM.

AT last there seemed some prospect of our being able for a time to " take things easy." Our rest at the Shan village had been very grateful to us; but somehow we had got so accustomed to be moving onward, that even our short halt had seemed a deplorable waste of time. Our thoughts were now all bent on home, and the way before us was still long and rough and beset by dangers. The canoe voyage was a new experience, and in some respects one of the most pleasant we had yet had. We had movement and progress—for our two slim little crafts, propelled by the dexterous strokes of the native boatmen, slipped through the water like fish; and at the same time we were relieved of the distressing toil that had hitherto taken up almost the whole of our energies. Our prows were pointing westward; the doctor told us, after consulting the pocket-compass which had so often been our " guide, philosopher, and friend," during the journey, that a straight line drawn in the course we were pursuing would, as nearly as he could calculate, carry us to the shores of " Merrie England " itself.

The thought inspired us with a wild wish to seize the paddles and put on a " spurt " for the old country ; we felt as if we could have flown over the hills and forests and waste places that intervened between us and the friends who were no doubt anxiously looking for news of us, and probably had, by this time, given us up for lost. But when we had made a practical trial of our proficiency in paddling, we were not long in discovering that we would best consult our own comfort and the rapid progress of the voyage by leaving the work entirely in the hands of the native canoemen.   Dr. Roland could ply a paddle almost as skilfully as the Canadian pioneers, in whose birch-bark canoes he had ascended and descended many a stream in the great North-West.   Hannibal's powerful arm was a splendid ally when " a long pull and a strong pull " was required.   But each had to admit that he was beaten hollow by the under-sized, spindle-legged canoemen whom we had engaged, and who seemed to have no more flesh on their bones than would make a respectable supper for one of the crocodiles that eyed us greedily from the water.   These men had been inured to this work from infancy, and had passed their whole lives on the rivers and creeks.   Their paddles struck the water with a finely-measured beat, while each sinew of their muscular frames, which were almost free from the encumbrance of clothes, stood out like whip-cord.

Away we skimmed like swallows up-stream, then, making excellent " time," while a beaded line of foam streamed away in our wake, and the " whish" of the canoes, as they sped through the water, sounded like an accompaniment to the musical but rather monotonous chant sung by our boatmen.   In the leading boat was the doctor, and with him Yung-wan and myself—the little Shan guide eagerly explaining and answering the questions of our chief as to the nature of the country ahead.   Tom and Hannibal were in charge of the second canoe.   The weather continued delightful—perhaps too warm in the mid-day hours for what would be considered pleasant picnicking at home ; but we had got well seasoned now to extremes of warmth and cold, and the sun could hardly blister our faces and hands to a darker hue than they already bore.   There were few indications of that break-up of the harvest weather and approach of winter which was one of our chief inducements in hurrying out of this country ; and the rain and hail storms, which were certain to overtake us if we waited for another week or two on the eastern side of the great range of hills for which we were bound, still held off.

We could therefore sit in our boats and enjoy the grand panorama which passed before us on either bank of the stream, and watch leisurely the strange aspects of

life in Further India which every new bend of the river
revealed to us. The tributary of the Mekong on which
we were voyaging would in Europe be considered an
important stream; yet on our return home we found
that not one of the maps of this country which we con-
sulted so much as indicated its existence. The French
expedition under Commander Lagrée had left the main
river some distance below the point where this affluent
—which we found was called the Me-Hem—entered
it; and Captain M'Leod and the other English travellers
who have penetrated a little way into this almost unknown region had also followed quite a different line
from that we were now pursuing.

The current in these lower reaches was deep and
smooth, and pretty free from sand and mud banks,
though occasionally our rowers had to exercise all their
skill to avoid running on shoals. Many of the inhabitants on its banks appeared to make their living by
fishing. Their tiny canoes were continually darting
across from bank to bank, or floating past us with the current; and judging from the quantities of queer-looking,
brilliantly-coloured fish which we saw lying at the bottom of the boats, they appeared to meet with excellent
sport—as likewise did the vast flocks of cranes, pelicans,
ibises, and other birds, that congregated on the trees or
swam about us in search of prey. Though we had taken
care to supply ourselves with rice and other stores for

the journey, at the village below, we did not disdain to
vary our fare by occasionally making a meal of the
slimy-looking finny creatures which the hospitable fishermen offered to us; or of a brace of wild ducks, when we
could secure that luxury without a waste of ammunition.
But I must confess that there was no tid-bit which we
relished so much as a broiled haunch of iguana, which a
venerable-looking native headman presented to us with
many *salaams;* and our sensations when the doctor the
same evening pointed out to us, on a branch, one of the
great, ugly, warty lizards, whose rich, juicy flesh we had
found so appetizing, were decidedly " queer."

From all the signs we saw around us, a numerous
population occupied this portion of the valley; and fishing was by no means the only or even the chief em-
ployment of the population.   The land for a considerable
distance back from the river-bank was cleared of forest,
and heavy crops, chiefly of rice, had just been reaped
from it.   Native hamlets, pagodas, and sharp-pointed
pyramids, which are so puzzling a feature of the architecture of this country, peeped out from the midst of
fine groves of nut-bearing and other fruit trees.   Here
and there were houses of larger dimensions, with gardens
and bath-houses opening out upon the river——doubtless the
seats of Burmese mandarins, Shan chieftains, or wealthy
Chinese merchants.   Flocks of well-fed cattle were to
be seen, and now and then a domesticated elephant; but

the work of the farm here, as in British India, seemed
to be chiefly performed by the buffalo. Large boats
passed us laden with rice, maize, buckwheat, and other
kinds of grain, or with piled-up cargoes of vegetables
and fruit for the markets on the Mekong. In some of
these vessels we saw Burmese pedlers seated by their
packages of cloth, crockery, and hardware goods, for
the most part, probably, of English manufacture, which
they were conveying down-stream, in order to be exchanged for the products of China and the Shan countries. I noticed with surprise among the wares of these
travelling merchants an article which seemed to be
guarded with peculiar care. It was none other than an
empty pale-ale bottle; and I think that even the most
rigid of water-drinkers would have hailed with delight
the sight of an object so common—perhaps too common—
in the old country, had he come upon it in so out-of-
the-way a locality as the valley of the Mekong.

I questioned Dr. Roland about it.

"There is no accounting for tastes," he replied.
"I understand that empty beer bottles have been the
'rage' for some time among the nobility and gentry of
this part of the world. No great man's reception-room
is thought properly furnished unless a pint bottle is stuck
up on the place of honour. All the shrines of Buddha
round about here have secured at least one of these
familiar specimens of English glass-work. The chief of

the Shan principality through which we are travelling
has lately been made happy by being able to complete a
set of a dozen of these bottles, which are ranged in a
line behind his throne of state, under the great brazen
gongs and the elephants' tusks which he esteems, next to
Bass's labels, as among his most precious and wonderful
possessions. It seems that these bottles and labels--are
believed here to represent the highest efforts of art as
practised among our benighted countrymen, and to be
executed with infinite labour and with the aid of
magic."

"What ridiculous people! What a funny craze!"
I remarked.

"Did you ever hear of the 'china craze' at home?"
asked the doctor, with some sarcasm in his tone. "I
forgot, however—there is one heirloom belonging to
the prince which he values more even than his beer
bottles. He is said to be the possessor of a magnificent
gem. On the question whether it is a diamond, or a
ruby, or an amethyst, or a sapphire, authorities differ;
but all agree that it is a jewel which has no peer in size
or in brilliancy in these parts. The place where it is concealed is kept a profound secret. If the prince's suzerain,
the King of Burmah, got an inkling of its whereabouts,
it would not be long in changing hands, for that despot
lays claim to all the precious stones that are found in his
dominions. Rumour has it that he would barter even

his white elephant—which you know has an official rank in the state only second to the king himself—for the Prince of Kiang-tong's jewel."

"Do you think there is any truth in the story?" asked I.

"That is more than I can say," rejoined Dr. Roland. "There is nothing impossible about it, and the country we are about to enter has been famous in all ages for its abundance in precious stones. I questioned Yung-wan, from whom I had most of the information I have given you, but he seemed disinclined to say much about the big brilliant, or, indeed, to talk at all on the subject of diamonds and diamond-mines. He peeped about him restlessly all the time we were speaking, as if he were afraid somebody might overhear us. I suspect that he has got into trouble at one time or other about smuggling jewels, and is afraid that some one will recognize him and rake up his old fault. They tell me that these Burmese packmen often carry much more valuable wares across the mountains than Manchester cottons, or even empty Bass and porter bottles—tiny little packets concealed about their persons containing gamboge, saffron, cardamoms, sandal-wood, and other precious drugs, spices, and dyes, or—who knows?—some gem of great price that has escaped the vigilant eyes of the Royal Proprietor of the Mines of Rubies and Sapphires. But," pursued the doctor, "as our dear old Scotch friend, Mr. Marshall, would have said—I wonder what he is doing at this moment, Bob!—this talk of princes and precious stones is 'neither here nor there.' We must put off our visit to his Highness of Kiang-tong—whose capital, Yung-wan tells me, is about a day's journey distant on our left —until our next trip into Further India. We have no time to spare at present to look on the glories of his gems or his row of bottles, or to listen to his grand orchestra of drums, gongs, cymbals, wind and string instruments, and Chinese swivel-guns. As for our friends the Burmese pack-merchants, I suppose you know what makes their presence here most significant to us?"

"Because," said I, "it shows that there is a track in this direction leading to British territory."

"Yes," my patron rejoined; "and a well-beaten one apparently. I regard the portion of our route we are now entering on as a very important and interesting one. The dividing chain between the Mekong and the Salwen River has never been crossed by any European in the latitude where we now are. It is a spur thrown off by the Himalaya, and runs down almost continuously from Thibet, where we crossed it a few weeks back, to Singapore, on the Strait of Malacca. It is almost unexplored, as I said; but you can see that a considerable trade is carried over its passes between the countries to the east and those on its western side. An excellent opening for British commerce might be found here. You remember

the strange-looking brown masses that you saw exposed
in the bazaar on the river, and which was sold in slices
to customers ?"

"I fancied it might be cheese, sir," said I. "But I
did not look at it closely, because it didn't appear nice."

"Cheese!" cried the doctor, highly amused. "Why,
man, that was tea—fermented tea. A budding planter
like you, Bob, should not have made a mistake like
that, more especially as the plant is of the Assam and
not the Chinese variety. It is grown on the drier hilly
parts here; and the leaf is reduced to a half-fermented
state, and packed into 'bricks.' The Burmese and the
natives fry it in oil, and use it as a kind of dessert. It
is the great treat here next to iguana flesh. There are
cotton and tobacco plantations, and the silk-worm is cultivated. The red clay that you saw is the famous stick-
lac out of which the Chinese, by a process that is kept
a strict secret, mould their marvellous lac-ware. It is
made of the ash of a kind of wood found in these forests.
But still more important, I think, are the signs of mineral wealth that are visible on every hand. You must
have noticed how plentiful copper ornaments and imple-
ments are; the very shares of the ploughs are made of
copper. I have seen specimens of iron ore that are the
richest I ever examined. There are also said to be mines
of gold, silver, tin, antimony, and cinnabar, not to mention the diamond-diggings."

Though I half suspected that Dr. Roland was partly poking fun at me, I own that this talk of hidden and untold wealth had a strangely exciting effect on me. I had visions of us all returning from our travels like Aladdin or Sinbad, with our pockets bulging out with precious stones.

"Couldn't we have a look about us for the diamond-mines—as we are here?" I asked in a tone that I fear betrayed my foolish and eager thoughts.

"No, Bob," answered my kind friend, laying his hand on my shoulder. "The 'Arabian Nights' are all at an end. The Valley of Diamonds and the Enchanted Cave are nowhere in this neighbourhood. My duty is to bring you safe and sound through the dangers into which, against my will, I have led you. As we cannot now-a-days employ a roc, genii, or a fiery griffin to take us up by the girdle and carry us over the tops of the mountains, but must plod most of the way on our legs, we have no time to spare for looking for diamonds, when we are more likely to catch fever. There is something far more valuable, however, which we may find in the direct path of duty."

"What is that, sir?"

"What would you say if we were to discover the true 'trade route to China,' about which so much has been written for generations past, and in quest of which so many regularly organized expeditions have set out in vain? I think," added the doctor, returning to his half-bantering tone, " if we bring back news of two new routes to the Flowery Kingdom, we will be entitled, not only to the thanks of the Geographical Society, but to those of the British Chambers of Commerce. But here at last come our friends, in time to break off this long harangue."

The conversation had taken place as we sat in our canoe in a still reach of the river, just above a place where it ran for a couple of hundred yards in a swift and rather broken current, which we had had no little ado in ascending. Yung-wan had gone to arrange for our taking up our quarters in a pagoda which rose close to the river-edge, and our crew had stretched themselves on the bank to rest after their exertions, leaving the doctor and me in charge of the boat. The second canoe, which was deeper in the water than ours, had fallen some distance behind; but just as we were beginning to get a little anxious for its appearance, we saw our companions in the gathering evening light beginning to take the current—it could hardly be called a rapid—with a will. On they came handsomely, the canoemen plying their paddles with all their might, and shouting their accustomed chorus until silenced by lack of breath. For some seconds the boat appeared to remain stationary, the vigorous strokes of the paddlers barely enabling it to hold its own against the violence of the stream. Then we heard Tom's voice endeavouring, in very bad time and tune, I admit, to raise " Rule Britannia " for the encouragement of his boatmates. The measure, however, was too slow, and the effect was not what it doubtless would have been had the crew been British tars. At last Hannibal struck in with one of the maddest and merriest of his " plantation dance " ditties, and the men responded to it as if electrified. " Hand over hand " the boat came up, breasting the current and sending the spray flying from its bows, and soon it was securely moored beside our own.

CHAPTER XV.

A HALT IN A PAGODA.

YUNG-WAN now approached with the news that he had arranged everything amicably with the monks; and as it was now quite chilly at night, even in these tropical latitudes, we lost no time in removing ourselves and our baggage to the pagoda. Ever since leaving the Mekong we had made some Buddhist "Kyoung" or temple our halting-place for the night, and in every case we had received kindly entertainment. These religious houses, indeed, serve the purpose of public inns in this country. The phoonghees, or priests, we found very different personages from their brethren in Thibet. Harsh fanaticism and savage zeal for the faith, which, perhaps, were fostered by the bleak prospects and biting arctic air of those lofty plateaux, did not well accord with the soft genial clime into which we had now descended. These phoonghees were lazy, easy-going people, who allowed their vows to sit very loosely upon them; and if they were quite capable of cheating and lying, they had clearly no mission for persecution like the lamas. Their features and even their garb indicated a milder temperament, and the very structure of the temples—light and airy, fantastically painted and gabled, and built of bamboos neatly joined together—presented the greatest possible contrast to the blind, gloomy, prison-like cells of stone in which the inmates of the lamissaries hide themselves. They were probably no better than they should be, and many of them, no doubt, led dissolute lives, but it could at least be said in their favour that they did not neglect the golden virtue of hospitality.

The old chief phoonghee, who now met us and escorted us to our sleeping-places for the night, was particularly gracious and communicative. He told us— what the aspect of the country during the last few hours' sail had led us to anticipate—that beyond this point, and until we reached the boundary of Burmah proper, we must not expect to find any more Buddhist monasteries with doors open to weary travellers. The cultivated land along the banks of the stream had gradually grown narrower, and patches of virgin forest now and then had intervened between the rice plantations. Instead of the marshes and alluvial plains lower down, hilly ridges began to hem in the valley and to throw out spurs to the banks of the stream. That evening's experience, too, had taught us that, in the most literal sense, our course would no longer be one of "smooth sailing."

The worthy chief phoonghee was pleased to take great interest in our journey—due perhaps to sundry little presents which we made him, not to mention the respectful manner which we invariably adopted towards these spiritual guides and the symbols of their national faith; and he concerned himself much about the lack of intellectual nourishment such as his order afforded, to which we would be condemned during our sojourn among the "savages." It troubled us much more, however, to learn that there was a prospect of our suffering from bodily hunger during the remainder of the journey; also, that we need no longer expect to find any protection in the "passport"—cut in Burmese characters on a slip of bamboo—which the doctor, by the expenditure of some of the last of his Indian rupees, had secured before setting out on the canoe voyage from the official who represented the Court of Mandalay. The important question of the means of transport was then discussed in all its bearings, Yung-wan, of course, acting as interpreter between us and our host. It seems that it was the practice for travellers bound westward to leave the stream at this place and hire mules, ponies, or oxen for the transmission of themselves and their baggage across the passes, under the protection of a guard. The circumstances at the present moment, however, were peculiar. The fighting that was going on within the Chinese frontier between the Imperialists and the

Mohammedan insurgents had unsettled the whole region. Large numbers of the Chinese population had fled across the border, which was within about a week's march from where we now were, and had thronged into the Shan villages to escape the impending massacres. Some of these refugees had found shelter in the very monastery under whose roof we were sitting. Rumours had come down within the last day or two that the Emperor's troops had defeated and scattered the rebel host, who, it was thought, would not unlikely also flee across the frontier for refuge.

This was rather disquieting news for us; we had no wish to stumble again on Akbar Khan in our travels. As the Chinese were again bundling up their effects and making preparations to return to their homes, baggage animals were scarcely to be had. The friendly old phoonghee also warned us that, if we followed the ordinary bridle-route leading to Mandalay and the Irrawady, we would be likely to land ourselves in trouble as soon as we reached the territory where the King of Burmah bears absolute sway, as Englishmen were at present in peculiarly bad odour with that monarch and his subjects. His advice was, that if we were determined to push on, we should continue to ascend the Me-Hem river as far as we could, and then endeavour to cross the mountains on foot, taking our chance of the "savages," who were, after all, more to be trusted than a Burmese guard. But

he considered that we ought to settle ourselves com-
fortably where we were for a few months until more
peaceful times should return, and in the interval he
should have time to thoroughly discuss with the doctor
the question of the duration of the "sixty-four great
Cycles of Time," the vanity and misery of human life,
and the illustrious virtues of the great Buddha, on all of
which topics he hoped to convert his guest to his own
way of thinking.

Dr. Roland, of course, declined, with many expressions
of thankfulness, this courteous offer. Even if we had
had time to waste, I fear that the prospect of having to
listen to the worthy old phoonghee's long and misty
"explanations" of his religious views would have made
us flee the hospitable roof of the kyoung, or at least
have made us often take advantage of that excellent rule,
inscribed among the two hundred and twenty-seven
Precepts of the order, which directs the monk "not to
preach the law to one lying down, unless sick." It was
settled, however, that, as to the route we should pursue,
we should follow his advice, which was urgently supported
by Yung-wan, and still more effectually by the discovery
that pack-animals could not be got at present for love or
for money.

As we had again before us the prospect of "roughing
it" for weeks to come, we indulged ourselves next morning
with a few hours' extra rest; and the head of the kyoung

and his assistants conducted us over their establishment,
pointing out with especial pride the little images of
silver, brass, marble, or jade, often with gems set in the
place of eyes, the lamps, candlesticks, fans, and other
offerings presented by the devout to the pagoda, among
which we were amused at observing the inevitable empty
beer bottle, a greasy tobacco pouch that had probably
found its way to the shores of Further India in some
sailor's pocket, and other equally humble and vulgar
European articles. More interesting to us was the library,
where we found a goodly collection of the sacred writ-
ings, mostly written in the ancient Pali language, introduced hither, with the religion, from Ceylon, and inscribed
on palm leaves, ivory tablets, or plates of copper, bound
together by cords. There were other manuscripts, from
which Dr. Roland was, by great favour, allowed to make
extracts and notes. By-and-by a troop of demure little
lads, with shaven heads, filed in for their daily lessons
—for these kyoungs are the public schools as well as the
places of entertainment in these countries—and we took
our departure. The yellow-robed monks accompanied
us to the river-bank, and warmly bade us farewell; and
we parted from them with a much more kindly feeling
towards the Buddhist priesthood and faith than we had
acquired in the highlands of Thibet.

Again afloat on the stream, we soon discovered that
its character and the appearance of the surrounding

country were rapidly changing. From a slow-flowing, navigable river, it was becoming a brawling mountain torrent; and the banks, no longer level and cultivated, were overhung by high cliffs and dense masses of forest. Still reaches of water were found at intervals, but these were becoming more rare. There was yet plenty of water for our canoes, but our upward course became a strenuous, unremitting struggle with the current. Often we had to land, and with ropes drag our canoes by main force up some piece of rushing, broken water which the paddlers could not face; and sometimes it was found necessary to haul our light craft on shore, and carry them bodily to the smoother water above the rapids. This was not an easy task; for where the bed of the stream was uncovered, it was strewn with great masses of rock, and where the forest approached close to the water's edge, it was next to impossible to cut and trample a way through the dense jungle and high grass. Now and then we came upon a native hut or two, of very humble construction, surrounded by a small clearing. By their features and dress, or rather want of dress, we recognized the owners of these shanties as the " savages" of whom the phoonghees had given us so unfavourable an account. But we found them mild, inoffensive people; and perhaps, as is the case elsewhere, they are regarded as barbarians merely for the reason that they are of alien race and customs. As Yung-wan did not understand their dialect, we did not profit from their counsels so much as we might have done; but we gathered from their gestures that there was danger about—whether from man or from wild beasts we could not make out —and that we should keep a strict watch against surprise.

The country grew more wild and broken, and also more beautiful. The forest around us especially became of grander proportions. Where high cliffs did not hem us in, the tall trees rose like a wall on either hand, shutting out the sky, except where the course of the stream opened up before us a vista, which frequently revealed glimpses of the lofty, saw-like peaks of the mountain mass to which we were bound, and which now seemed wonderfully close at hand. Or I might compare the towering trunks and overhanging foliage of these noble trees to the columns and roof of a stately and solemn cathedral aisle. Only here everything was of Nature's workmanship, and she displayed a variety of form and gorgeousness of colouring in her work which man cannot hope to approach. The stems and branches of the trees were draped with the most beautiful mosses and ferns. Some were of tiny and delicate structure, while we saw specimens of a kind of "staghorn" fern, whose fronds were four or five feet in length. Magnificent orchids also attached themselves to the bark; and it is impossible to describe the richness and brilliancy of the

tints displayed by this the most splendid of all the orders of flowering plants. High aloft, where the sunlight glimmered on the tops of the monarchs of the forest, many species of tropical birds fluttered about and repeated their calls to each other, the grating harshness of their notes being strangely in contrast with their gorgeous feathers. Sometimes a little sun-bird or some other bright-plumaged creature would dart down after an insect into the gloom of the forest below, the metallic gleam of its crest and throat shining like a spark in the darkness. Troops of monkeys also gambolled about at a safe elevation, and seemed to take immense interest in our movements, leaping along from branch to branch by our sides, and occasionally scurrying down the trunks in order to take a nearer view of the intruders through the leaves or between the rocks. The slightest gesture on our part sent these scouts darting like lightning up again among the higher branches, where they joined their mates in angry screaming, chattering, and expostulating, which, I daresay, if it could have been interpreted, would have made us heartily ashamed of the impropriety of our conduct. The heavy thud of a large nut on the ground told us that, if we were to venture on shore, the monkey objections to our presence would be hammered into our stupid human skulls in a more impressive way.

Radiant butterflies, with the most elegantly formed wings and lovely markings, fluttered over the stream, or hovered from flower to flower on the banks. In the evening, moths that rivalled their noonday-loving brethren in beauty came forth; and the burnished, scaly coats of innumerable species of insects of the beetle tribe fairly blazed in the shadow. Nowhere had we seen tropical nature under such alluring aspects, and never had we had such opportunity of adding to our knowledge. But, alas! we could only gaze longingly and pass on. No time could now be spared for botanizing or for insect-collecting; and we did not know what unseen dangers might be lurking for us in the thicket. The labour of forcing our way up-stream occupied almost our whole energies; and the touches of fever from which each of us suffered also impaired our enjoyment of the scenery.

Our canoes "brought up" in a little pool in the stream, where the deep reach of water was surrounded by steep cliffs screened by masses of vegetation so dense that only here and there the dark rock revealed itself behind the curtain of green. Graceful trees, many of them bearing fruit, others covered with blossom, grew in the most inaccessible places, and their leaves and branches were reflected in the calm surface of the pool. Climbing-plants crept and wound themselves everywhere, and wove the whole into one matted web of greenery. A lovelier spot we had not yet reached in our travels; and we rested a little to enjoy the scene, and finding the place suitable, decided to camp here for the night.

"Wouldn't they give us something if we could carry off this scene bodily and set it down in Kew Gardens?" remarked Tom admiringly. "Why, it would take the scientific fellows weeks, I suppose, to classify the new plants. And wouldn't stay-at-home folks stare? They have no notion of the splendid things that there are in the world, and they won't believe us when we tell about them."

"And wouldn't we give something for a glimpse, even for a second or two, of the sights that every day meet the eyes of those 'stay-at-home' folks that you speak of so scornfully?" asked Dr. Roland. "I am sure that for a sprig of hawthorn, for the scent of an English meadow with daisies and buttercups, or for a sight of a breezy hill-side covered with gorse and fragrant with heather and thyme, you would gladly surrender all this gorgeous blaze of green and gold, if not even your supper."

Hannibal, who was engaged in preparing our well-earned meal, by dexterously cooking over the embers a couple of jungle-fowl, looked up and shook his head. But Tom and I clapped our hands approvingly; and the doctor proceeded,—

"These gaudy hussies of flowers that stare at us so impudently are no more to be compared with the shy, sweet wildings at home than the croaking, screaming dandies of parrots overhead are to be likened to our own larks or thrushes; ay, Tom, or your mandarin's daughter to one of the girls of our tight little island.'

"I have often wished myself," said Tom, "that we
might come across a good honest nettle or bramble.
Still, sir, you must allow that this is very grand and
beautiful."

"Very beautiful indeed," returned the doctor; "though
to my mind freshness and sweetness and simplicity are
best. Come; we are not so badly off after all. Here
is Hannibal with our fowls done to a turn. I think we
will find these as palatable as if they were home-grown
poultry—which are supposed to be the descendants of
this wild breed—and to have quite a 'gamey' flavour in
addition."

Yung-wan, who had been absent for a couple of hours,
now approached, nimbly making his way towards us
through the undergrowth and over the rocks. He had
been out on the scouting duty in which he had
shown himself so skilled, and he reported that above
us, at a distance of little more than a quarter of a mile,
was a village inhabited by Shans and Danoos, a tribe
speaking a broken dialect of Burmese. After carefully
reconnoitring, he had ascertained that the inhabitants
were peaceable and well-disposed, and he had arranged
with the headman for our obtaining quarters for the
night.

Having finished our meal, we again proceeded up-
stream, and reached the village as night was closing in.
Just a week had elapsed since we had left the Mekong.

CHAPTER XVI.

A TRAMP THROUGH THE FOREST.

E slept soundly on the hard matting spread for us in the guest-chamber of the headman's house; but next morning we were early astir. The first thing that was made plain to us, was that we must now bid adieu for the time to our canoeing experiences. For the last stage or two the river-journey had seemed to us rather more toilsome and troublesome than a march by land. Where we were not straining against the current, we were carrying our boats and baggage over stock and stone—"thorough bush, thorough brier." And such bushes for denseness, and briers for the length and sharpness of their thorns! On the whole, we were not disappointed to find that, beyond this point, it would be impossible at this season of the year to make any progress by water.

The village where we were now resting was one of the halting-places of the traders, who on their land journeying here struck the river and followed its banks

for some distance on their way to the mountain passes
and to Burmah. We, of course, assumed that we
should pursue the same track, more especially as the
headman declared that the only known crossing-place of
the range lay in this direction. Yung-wan, however,
took our leader aside, and assured him that he knew of
a much safer and more suitable path, which could be
reached by ascending a small stream that fell into the
Me-Hem at this spot. Certainly the outlook in the
direction pointed out by the guide was not very inviting.
The banks of the little tributary, which was hardly larger
than a brook, were clothed with thick primeval forest,
which looked as if it had never been trodden by human
foot; while a well-defined path led up the main valley,
and the wood there appeared to be much more thin and
penetrable. The doctor, however, had complete confidence in our guide's faithfulness and skill. The stories
of refugee bandits and rebels from Chinese territory
having sought shelter in this wild district were repeated
to us in more definite form. They were supposed to be
lying in wait to pounce upon any party venturesome
enough to attempt to cross the pass, and for several
days no one had dared to make the journey. All things
considered, we thought it preferable to take our chance
of being lost in the forest and eaten up by wild beasts,
rather than run the risk of falling again into the hands
of Akbar Khan and his associates.

The headman of the village expressed great astonishment when he heard of our resolve. He assured us that the jungle paths in the direction in which we proposed to go all ended within a few miles of the spot where we stood, and were only used by hunters. Nothing was known of the forest-covered country beyond, except that it extended to the foot of mountains that were, quite inaccessible. In his view, the only alternatives were, remaining where we were, or returning by the road whence we had come. Yung-wan, however, continued confident, and the doctor obdurate to all the arguments of the "local authority." We shouldered our guns and knapsacks—very light they were, as beseemed people setting out on such a journey; but the doctor's note-book, which I had rescued "under fire," was not forgotten—bade farewell to our friends of the village, and to our boat crew, who had proved such willing and trusty workers, and plunged into the dark and lonesome forest.

It was some time before the silence and monotony of our surroundings began to impress themselves upon us. We were rather elated at being once more our own masters. Again we were thrown entirely on our own resources, and our spirits rose as we thought that we were dependent on our own legs and wills, and not upon the whims of a tropical torrent, for the route we should pursue. Not that we had much choice in the matter of a road. Numerous paths, indeed, led through the bamboo

jungle and grass immediately surrounding the village
fields; but the tracks piercing the taller forest beyond
were hard to find and difficult to follow.   It is true that
we could not stray far either to the right hand or the
left; generally we were hemmed in by walls of inter-
twined stems, branches, and leaves, sometimes composed
of saw and razor edged grasses and barbed thorns, so
thickly set that there hardly seemed room for a snake to
wind its way through.   That serpents did manage to pay
visits to the pathway, we had frequently unpleasant re-
minders; and we had to keep a sharp watch lest we
should place a foot on some slimy poisonous wretch that,
on hearing our approach, was slowly trailing himself into
cover, looking all the more wicked and ugly, we thought,
for the rainbow sheen on his scaly hide.   A much
greater obstacle, however, was found in the fallen branches
and twisted roots that stretched across the path, and
over which we were continually stumbling, while a cold
shudder would run through one as the thought occurred
that at last a snake had been trodden upon.   Spiders'
webs, as big, as Tom remarked, as " small cables "—or
at least, almost of the thickness of cotton thread—extended across the pathway, and were strong enough to
give a sharp blow when we incautiously ran our noses
against them in the obscurity.   The proprietors of these
gigantic cobwebs we often noticed lurking among the
leaves by the wayside, and watching, like patient fisher-

men, for what fortune might bring into their nets. Great, bloated, wicked-looking ogres they looked, with bodies as large as walnuts, and sprawling legs six inches in length. We had little difficulty in believing the stories that travellers have told about tiny sun-birds building their nests in the abandoned webs of these monsters.

Our track seemed to have been more trodden by wild beasts—elephants, rhinoceroses, and other bulky creatures —than by man. It brought us by-and-by to the banks of the little stream whose valley we were ascending; and after following it for some distance, it turned again into the woods. The trees gradually became of larger dimensions, and the undergrowth disappeared. We were in the primeval forest, where the axe of the wood-cutter had never sounded. We could breathe more freely, for we were no longer hedged in by grass and jungle. The trodden path grew more and more faintly marked, and at length was lost. We could pursue our way in any line we chose; for, in spite of the air-roots and climbing-plants that hung around each giant of the forest, like the guys and ratlins about a ship's mast, passage seemed to be indifferently open to us in every direction. The mighty stems of different species of palms and other trees, measuring sometimes thirty or forty feet in girth, towered aloft to a height that strained our eyes when we looked up. We felt mere insects in size as we wound around and between these immense

trunks, or like a party of Liliputians who had wandered
into a forest of Brobdingnag.   Twilight gloom and
solemn stillness reigned here, though a storm might be
raging without, or the sun of the tropics shining ver-
tically down on the thick mass of foliage overhead.
Here and there a gleam of sunshine found its way down
through the branches, like a ray from a bull's-eye lan-
tern, scattering bright flecks of light on the boles and
roots of the great trees, or on the sodden, leaf-strewn
ground over which we marched.   At intervals a patch
of blue sky might be seen overhead.   This was where
some hoary veteran of the forest had fallen in the ranks
from old age and decay at the roots, and lay prostrate
on the ground, or hung suspended by the innumerable
lianas and lialines that united it with the other trees,
which, one might fancy, were in the act of lowering
their old companion slowly into its grave.   When we
reached one of these prostrate stems, we were glad to
make a halt for rest, and also to examine the rare and
lovely things with which it was generally covered.   The
rough bark was a kind of "mosaic work" of lichens,
mosses, and ferns, and each high branch that had caught
the sun had been made the adopted home of delicate
flowering parasites that would have stocked a conservatory.   Beetles and other boring insects with shiny
coats of mail had perforated the rotten wood in all directions; and in the midst of our most interesting inves-

tigations, we were sometimes put to ignominious flight by the colonies of ants that had taken possession of the decaying trunk. Still more unpleasant were the attentions which sundry black, wriggling scorpions seemed anxious to bestow on us when we disturbed them in their quarters under the bark or the leaves; and once I checked my hand just in time, as I was about to examine a beautiful object, which turned out to be the green and spotted body of a small poisonous snake. It was clear that among the tree-tops, a hundred and fifty feet overhead, there was a world of life, full of movement, light, and colour; and we were tempted to wish that we had wings like the birds, or nimble limbs like the monkeys, that we might spend our time up there instead of crawling through the dismal shades below.

On leaving these sunny spots, the gloom of the forest seemed deeper than before, and the utter solitude and sameness of the interminable vistas of trees confused and depressed us. Yung-wan, however, was perfectly in his element. He picked out the easiest way with unerring instinct, and had apparently complete confidence in his power to guide us through this labyrinth. A haunting fear that we were being watched or tracked, however, seemed to possess him. He glanced suspiciously around him for signs of danger; and often made us halt, in order that he might make a detour back upon the way we had come, and discover whether we were being followed.   Yung-wan, since his adventure with the rebels, had got "ambuscades on the brain." Nothing occurred to justify these precautions; and, for ourselves, we felt certain that it was impossible that any enemy could have been tracking us up without revealing ere this time some sign of his presence.

Hitherto we had come across very few of the big game of the region.   Plenty of foot-tracks and other signs of elephants, tigers, and rhinoceroses had been observed, but we had only caught momentary glimpses of these large animals in the flesh.   This was perhaps lucky both for them and for us.   We had no wish to expend our small remaining stock of ammunition in shooting them for mere sport; and so long as other sources of food supply held out, we were well enough satisfied that the wild beasts should give us a "wide berth."   Now the guide halted at a small rivulet with steep rocky banks, which ran like a deep gash through the forest.   There was a crossing-place over the stream which bore marks of having been often used by the heavy forest animals. Yung-wan listened intently, and made a sign for us to remain perfectly still.   Was the mysterious "enemy" about to make his long-expected spring on us?   We hearkened attentively, but for some moments heard nothing except the rushing of the brook.   At last we thought we heard a sound of snapping branches, and the noise soon became quite distinct.   Under Yung-wan's direction we concealed ourselves carefully behind a mass of rocks and shrubs near the ford, and awaited the issue. The sound of breaking twigs and heavy footfalls drew nearer; and now and then came a grunt or a trumpeting note that alone would have told us that a troop of elephants was approaching. Soon the broad forehead of an enormous "tusker" appeared. His trunk was carried high in air, and he proceeded deliberately and carefully to reconnoitre the position before advancing. The elephant stretched out his long proboscis to right and left, and blew great clouds of steam from it with a dissatisfied air. Evidently he scented danger—perhaps, like our guide, he was troubled in mind about ambuscades—but could not make out where it lay. Had he known that four guns were bearing upon him at a distance of not many yards away, he would have been even more ill at ease. A breeze was blowing down the ravine, and we had taken care to ensconce ourselves to leeward of the crossing-place, so that he could not get the "wind" of us. After flapping his ears doubtfully, and taking a nervous glance around with his small eyes, he made up his mind that the fancied danger was a delusion. His body emerged from out the thicket, and as he leisurely picked his way down the broken bank and across the stones forming the bed of the rivulet, we had a capital view of him. A splendid fellow he was, standing at least ten and a half feet high, and bearing an enormous pair of tusks. Close behind him came two female elephants, and a young half-grown male, and another female, with her " baby," brought up the rear. It was only a small family party whose passage we were privileged to see, and we looked on with interest, but without seeking to disturb them. It was curious to watch the attention bestowed on the baby elephant by its mother, and the anxiety she showed that it should keep pace with the elder members of the party. It exhibited some reluctance to descend to the brook, so she gently pushed it from behind with her trunk, and then carefully guided its stumbling steps up the other slope.

When the last of this interesting group had disappeared into the forest, and before the cracking of branches that marked their progress had ceased to be heard, we resumed our march. We began to discover that small streams running through deep gullies at right angles to our course formed a feature of this forest country. Between these water-courses the ground heaved up in ridges, which became steeper and higher as we advanced. The wood here was not so dense and high as that which we had passed through, and presently we reached a glade on the summit of one of the ridges which gave us a prospect of what lay ahead. The country around us had the appearance of a tossing sea of forests, that rose in higher and higher billows until it seemed to roll itself to the foot of a lofty precipitous mountain wall, that ex-

tended, as far as our eyes could see, right across our path,
and was now so close at hand that, with the sun beginning
to set behind it, its shadow already fell on us. We could
see, where the green ocean of verdure dashed itself against
these cliffs, that masses and lines of trees climbed high
up among the rocks, like the spray of a broken wave;
but above, all looked "dark, substantial, black," in the
fast-descending twilight.

We were too tired to discuss the problem of how this
formidable obstacle was to be surmounted; so we made
ourselves comfortable where we were, and in a few
minutes were sleeping the sleep of exhaustion and of a
good conscience. The morning, perhaps, would bring
more light and better counsel.

CHAPTER XVII.

THE LOST CITY.

THE morning, however, did not bring us all the comfort that we could have wished. The first object that caught our waking eyes was the great wall of mountains standing before us grim and immovable. Its aspect was indeed changed from that of the previous evening, for the sun was now shining brightly on its scarred and wrinkled front. "Beaked promontories" ran out from the main mass of rock, and its sides were ploughed with deep ravines. Some of these might possibly afford a passage by which the crags might be scaled, but they did not look promising at a first view.

"I suppose this is the outer buttress of the Tanen-Toung-gyee Mountains," said the doctor, after a quiet survey. "I should like to know how Yung-wan proposes to get us across."

The guide was engaged in his usual preliminary round of inspection, and we could see him on an elevation some little distance off carefully scanning the landmarks.

"I wonder that the Shans and Burmese should take the trouble to invent so long and ugly a name," remarked Tom, whose dissatisfied mood was probably explained by his having had no breakfast. "I should not be surprised at any enormity that the Chinese or the Thibetans would commit in the matter of names; but our friends down below are easy-going, sensible people, and really 'Tanen-Toung-gyee' is too absurd a title to give to their principal range of mountains."

"I think we might get over the name, if we could only get over the fact," answered the doctor quietly. "I am afraid that is only the first step in the ascent that we see opposite to us; and if there are many like it, our muscles and our patience will be well tried before we get to the top. But why this sudden gush of tenderness towards the Shans and the Burmese, Tom? Is it because in your present famished state you are fondly remembering the lean chicken and the mess of rice which you helped to consume at the headman's hospitable board yesterday morning? An active young man of healthy appetite like you should not be above breakfasting on fruit, when nothing better is to be had; and at this moment I have my eye on the very choicest fruit that the tropics can produce."

"Where?" cried Tom, jumping to his feet, while the other members of the "expedition" also showed sudden alacrity.

The doctor pointed to some tall trees, of a different tint of green than those immediately surrounding them, on the slope overhanging the stream below us. In a few minutes, by scrambling and slipping down the steep bank, and at the cost of sundry rents in our already ragged clothes, we were standing under the shade of the grove that had allured us from afar. The prevailing tree had a stately, tapering stem rising to a height of over a hundred feet, and surmounted by a shapely dome of leaves. At that great height we could descry dusky masses of fruit of most tempting appearance glimmering among the branches. There was no need, however, to climb so high to reach them, even if the feat had been within our power, for the fruit was ripe, and the ground was thickly strewn with bronze-coloured globes larger than oranges. Dr. Roland picked up a specimen and handed it to Tom; but no sooner had that young hero removed the tough, leathery rind, and carried a portion of the creamy pulp under his nose, preparatory to conveying it to his stomach, than an expression half-puzzled, half-disgusted came over his features. He withdrew the tempting-looking morsel from his lips, and looked reproachfully at our leader, as if he suspected that a practical joke was being played on him.

"Eat it up, man," said Dr. Roland. "Never mind the smell—or the stink, if so you choose to consider it."

Tom, impelled by a keen appetite, again boldly approached the fruit to his lips; and immediately on tasting it, his expression changed to one of ineffable enjoyment.

"What is it, sir?" asked I, who, with Hannibal, now became anxious to try the experiment in which Tom Wilson was finding such absorbing satisfaction.

"It is the durian," our friend replied, "the undisputed monarch of tropical fruits. I had no idea that it grew in so high a latitude as this, though it is common enough in the Malay Peninsula, to the south of us. But try it for yourselves."

-None of us seemed to receive exactly the same impression of the taste of this regal fruit, but all agreed that it was delicious and indescribable. As the rich pulp, of the consistency and appearance of custard, melted away in our mouths, we seemed to detect all the fruity juices and flavours that had ever visited our palates combined into delectable union. The strangest thing about it, however, was the peculiar, half-fragrant, half-putrid odour that assailed our nostrils. If the palate was more than satisfied, the nose was more than dubious about the merits of this luscious banquet.

"Well, lads, what do you think of your breakfast? Has pear or pine-apple or peach any chance with this quintessence of sweets?" asked the doctor.

"Certainly not," said Tom enthusiastically.

"Except in one respect," I ventured to add.

"Ah, yes! to be sure there is that queer smell. A traveller has compared it to the stench of a bad sewer as felt through a perfumed pocket-handkerchief."

"I think there is more of the sewer than the perfume about it."

"Perhaps there is," was the doctor's response. "Well, Bob, there is nothing quite perfect in this world. Even the durian has its weak point; but after all it is an exquisite fruit, and almost worth, as somebody has said, the trouble of making a voyage to the East in order to taste it. The rich dinner-givers in London would give a handsome sum for that fine ruddy fellow you hold in your hand; but it will not endure being carried half so far."

"What would the bench of Aldermen give to be sitting under this tree!" said Tom, waxing eloquent, as he proceeded to divest another durian of its stiff, burnished skin. "The Lord Mayor himself, I believe, would leave his chair and his calipash and calipee, and exchange his robes of scarlet for my ragged jacket, if he could only get into my shoes this instant. I appeal to this honourable assembly. I address you, sir, and my learned friend Mr. Robert Brown, and the honourable and gallant namesake of the illustrious Carthaginian general; and I ask if you can imagine a more tranquil spot, or a more perfect picture of enjoyment."

The orator was interrupted by a rough and sudden

push administered by the doctor's hand, that sent him and the durian rolling over and over for two or three yards. A second after, a great round mass from the branches overhead fell with a heavy thud, and made a deep dint on the very spot where the self-satisfied youth had been seated. Had he not been thrown so unceremoniously off his balance, he would certainly have been stunned, perhaps seriously hurt, by the heavy fruit falling from so great a height on his head.

We lost no time in moving away from this attractive but rather dangerous spot. Yung-wan was signalling to us from the ridge above, and as he was eager to make a start, we were, half an hour later, again trudging up-hill and down-hill, through brake and forest, at the heels of our little guide.

Some change was now made in the direction we were pursuing. Instead of making straight for the high mountains we had seen in front, Yung-wan "edged off" a little towards the south. A long day's march lay before us, and we were soon tired enough of toiling up the narrow valleys of mountain streams, varied only by stiff climbs over hilly spurs covered with jungly forest and down into the stony bed of another torrent. Each time we caught a peep through the thicket of the range, it loomed a little higher and nearer; but considering how close at hand it looked on the previous evening, it appeared desperately hard to reach. If they had not seemed so solidly

planted on their foundations, one might have fancied
that the mountains were fleeing as we pursued, and that
we were only making up on them after a long stern-chase.

We now entered a wider valley, between hills that
could be made out to be spurs thrown off directly by
the main range.   Something else caught our attention,
but for some time we hesitated to credit our own eyes.
Could these chisellings on the rocks and these hewn
slabs, forming a kind of broken causeway underfoot,
actually be signs of the presence and handiwork of man
in the heart of what we had believed to be an unexplored
wilderness ?   But the races that now inhabit this region
have neither the inclination nor the skill to construct the
works whose remains we saw scattered about us.   Their
efforts at house architecture are represented by flimsy
huts of bamboo, bound together by ratans, or at most
wooden temples for their idols, covered with grotesque
carvings.   Their roads are mere trails through the
forest, for which, probably, they were originally indebted
to elephants and buffaloes.   But the race who had con-
ceived and executed the vast labours with which this
lonely valley was strewn, must have been of the "sons of
Anak"—people with a purpose, belonging to an earlier
age and to a higher civilization than their degenerate
successors of to-day.   The doctor had little doubt, from
an examination of the remains, that we had stumbled
on the ancient site of a settlement of that mysterious

people, the Khmers, whose ruined cities and temples, buried in the depths of the forests of Cambodia and Siam, are among the chief marvels of the East.

Excited by our discovery, we pushed rapidly on, in spite of the guide's injunctions to be cautious. The causeway which we followed, though crumbling away and broken in many places, and with long grass and shrubs growing in the interstices of the stones, afforded a more smooth and easy road than any we had trod for many a long day. The traces of ancient occupation and decayed grandeur grew more numerous. Everything bore the impress of extreme antiquity; and from all we saw, no one might have visited this forsaken spot for a thousand years or more. The massive slabs of stone under foot were worn with the friction of water. Masses of earth and crumbling bricks had slipped down the sides of the valley and obstructed the path. Heavy blocks of stones, which had evidently formed the foundations on which the brick superstructure had been built, still for the most part held their positions, though in some places the site of the ruins was nearly obliterated by dense masses of thorns and creeping-plants. These works had, from their position and form, been built for defensive purposes; and when they were entire, and manned by the energetic race that had constructed them, no enemy could possibly have approached their stronghold. There were many places in the valley and on the hills that confined it which were suited for cultivation, and before scrub and forest were allowed to overgrow the rich soil of this district, it must have supported a teeming population.

Clambering over a pile of masonry, we came in full view of an amphitheatre of cliffs, enclosing in their embrace the ruins of the "Lost City." The tall, sombre crags were beginning to cast long shadows, and beneath them was a chaos of huge mounds and walls, shattered and tottering towers, broken monuments, and colossal statues that had been hurled from their pedestals, and above which now waved mournfully the dark plumes of a rank jungle vegetation. These thorns and evil weeds were now the only traces of life in this once busy scene, and they only deepened the feeling of utter desolation which it produced on our minds. As we advanced into the midst of the ruins, our amazement and our sense of oppressive loneliness increased. We passed through long and wide courtyards, paved with brick and stone, and strewn with fragments of beautifully carved columns and capitals, and bas-reliefs of gods and warriors and dancing-girls. Leading from these were flights of broad steps, now dismantled and broken, and overgrown with weeds, and spacious avenues lined with gigantic figures of man and beast. Here the head of a sculptured elephant or the grinning face of a stone tiger or dragon peered out from under the overhanging branches, and a few paces further the form of a giant lay prone among the rubbish, with his great club, broken short off, lying beside him. What struck us much was the contrast which the rude design and execution of these misshaped monsters presented to the delicacy and taste of the ornaments with which the buildings were covered. Further on, confused piles of masonry, the ruins of former palaces and temples, blocked our way. Underneath, some of the doorways and chambers were almost complete; but nearly all the towers had fallen, and the great blocks of granite and ironstone were tilted and poised in every conceivable position. The giant creepers that grew between the stones, and clung and twisted with their long roots and branches over the buildings in every direction, like the twining bodies of, boa-constrictors, had helped to complete the ruin. There had been more, however, than the hand of man and of time engaged in the work of destruction. It looked as if some terrible earthquake had shaken down the sacred fanes on the heads of the worshippers, and buried the proud lords of this mysterious city under the ruins of their palaces.

We sought shelter in a spacious chamber in what appeared to be the principal temple, which had risen close beneath the brow of the rock, and resolved to delay till the morrow making a close examination of the ruins. It was some time, however, before our excitement and

the strangeness of our surroundings would allow us to
sleep, and we talked long into the night, chiefly in
unprofitable conjectures as to what manner of people
they had been who had raised these wonderful structures, and what kind of life they could have led in
this secluded valley, before the mysterious calamity had
occurred that drove them forth from the shelter of their
cyclopean walls. The beasts of the night also seemed
to have all awakened and to be calling to each other
with weird howlings and shrieks, and great bats flitted
about our room with an eerie sound. One could have
imagined that the spirits of the ancient inhabitants had
been aroused out of their long sleep, and were questioning
one another as to the strange visitors from the world of
the living who had invaded their city of the dead.

We were early afoot in the morning, however, and
made considerable progress in taking measurements of
the ruins. We found them even more extensive and
elaborate than we had supposed on the previous evening.
The temple especially in which we had passed the night
had been a stupendous and beautiful structure. We
ascended the remains of an outer staircase of stone, and
thus getting on the top of the ruined edifice, made our
way with difficulty and danger, sometimes along the
crumbling edges of walls, and through vast dilapidated
halls, till we found ourselves close to the rock which
formed part of the precipice that girded in the valley.

The other members of the party were a little in front
of Hannibal, who lingered behind to peep into some
dark corridors that attracted his notice. A shout of
alarm from the negro brought the rest of us to his side.
His eyes were rolling nervously in their sockets, and as
soon as he could get breath he whispered, in terrified
accents, that he had seen the form of a man disappear
down a gloomy passage which seemed to lead away into
the interior of the building.

This was disturbing news, and Yung-wan's yellow
face, I thought, turned to a wan ash colour with alarm.
We questioned Hannibal closely as to what he had really
seen, as he seemed to be a little confused, and we knew
that, though brave as a lion in other respects, he was
not above the influence of superstitious fear.

"Saw um plain, Massa Doctah," he protested earnestly,
"saw um clear as mud."

"Why didn't you catch hold of him?"

"Hi! flopped out o' sight, right b'hind dat dar wobbling
t'ing," answered Hannibal, still in a state of great excitement, and pointing to a hideous stone griffin which
guarded the low entrance of the passage. "Couldn't
have ketched hold o' a ghost anyhow!" he added reproachfully.

"What was he like? Was he in the native dress?"

"No; not like de niggah fellahs round yere—'spect-
ably dressed man like myself." As honest Hannibal's

cotton jacket was now a thing of shreds and patches, and his knees and brawny calves revealed themselves freely through his trousers, his notions of being "respectably dressed" were not extravagant.

"Have you ever seen anybody like him before?"

"No, Massa Doctah," returned the negro, slowly pondering, as if he were recalling one by one the features of the mysterious stranger, and trying to find resemblances. "Nebber seen anybody a bit like him."

"Would you know the face if you were to meet it again?"

"No," said Hannibal gravely, scratching his wool; then brightening up a little, "I wouldn't know de *face;* but I would know de *back,* if I met *it.*"

"Then you saw only his back?"

"Only de back, sar," was the reply received by the astonished doctor, while we could not help bursting into a laugh at this result of the cross-questioning

Meantime a light had been kindled, and we stooped and entered the dark portal, under the outstretched wings and yawning jaws of the griffin. It was not a corridor after all; only a recess in the wall, which contained nothing except a few large vampire bats, which came flapping against our light with a suddenness that made our hearts jump to our mouths. At the farther end, however, was a wide crack, where the walls had been rent apart, and it was just possible that a man night have squeezed himself through this opening. We ried the aperture by turns, and it was found that only Yung-wan's supple form could by any possibility get hrough. If any one evilly disposed towards us were n hiding on the other side, the guide would have been completely at his mercy had he attempted alone to explore the dark chamber with which the "crack in the wall" seemed to communicate, and we would have been unable to render him any aid.

It was thought best, therefore, not to prosecute the search further ; and it seemed so improbable that another human being could be in this hidden spot besides ourselves, and so hard to believe that anybody could escape by the narrow cranny in the wall, that we almost succeeded in persuading one another, and even Hannibal, that he must have mistaken the flutter of a bat's wings for the vanishing form of a man. The incident had, however, made us all uneasy; and we became more eager to leave the "lost city" behind us than we had a little ago been to explore all its secret recesses.

Rising above the other ruins were the remains of what had once been a lofty tower of singular proportions. A great part of it was still standing, shattered and crumbling, but strong even in its decay; the grotesque carvings with which the outer walls were covered for the most part still retained their positions. It was Dr. Roland's opinion that this was probably the greatest of

the " high places " in which the idolaters who built the
pile had worshipped, as it was their custom to have the
" holy of holies " in their temples as near as possible to the
light of day and the influence of the stars. To this part
of the ruins the guide led us, and proceeded to wind his
way upwards through dusty galleries and narrow stair-
cases, where the only light sometimes was what trickled
in by apertures in the walls and roof, and where we occasionally had to crawl on hands and knees to surmount
the heaps of rubbish. Rather unexpectedly, we emerged
into the daylight on a platform on the side of the mountain. Near us was a low doorway in the cliff, and into this
Yung-wan dived without hesitation. Of course we had
to follow. Stooping low, in case we should strike our
heads against the projections on the roof, we slowly
groped our way upwards through the rock-hewn passage
for what appeared a terribly long space of time. Then
again we greeted the light of the sun, on a second platform much higher up the cliff than the first. Here we
found steps cut in the rock, which ascended in zigzags
towards the summit of the mountain. A heavy block of
stone lay close to the dark portal from which we had
emerged. Yung-wan made a narrow examination of the
ground, and appeared reassured by what he saw; and, at
his request, we assisted in rolling the boulder against the
mouth of the archway.

Pausing now for a little, to fetch breath, we began the

ascent of the mountain. Though the steps were deeply cut, and our hold made secure by iron pins which had been driven into the rock at the more dangerous places, this part of our task was no easy one. As the least robust of the party, I had several times to rest a few minutes to get my "wind," and to take another look down upon the marvellous and mysterious scene we were leaving.

"Come away, Massa Bob," said trusty Hannibal, reaching out a hand to help me along. "Jest think you're gwine upstairs to dinnah."

"It must be dinner in a light-house then, or at the top of a factory stalk," put in Tom.

"Say we are climbing the steps of the temple of Fame at once," cried Dr. Roland, who was, with the guide, some paces ahead. "Forward, lads! here is the top of the mountain in sight at last."

CHAPTER XVIII.

THE GREAT SAPPHIRE.

"CAN you make out yet whereabout we are, and whither we are going?" asked Tom.

"No, Tom," replied Dr. Roland, knitting his brows, on which for several days an expression of anxiety had sat, which did not escape our notice. "No, I can't make it out—exactly," he repeated, as he put away his pocket-compass, which he had been consulting as he narrowly scanned the hills and valleys around and below us.

Nine days had elapsed since we had left the Mekong—six spent in canoeing on the tributary stream, and three in marching on foot through the jungle and forest; but judging by our worn frames and tattered clothes, it might have been supposed that we had been as many months on the tramp. We were literally in rags; and this was a serious matter, when the chill, broken weather was setting in, and when we had again ascended into cold, high mountainous regions. The journey had been toilsome and monotonous,—on the river, constantly struggling against the current, or hauling our canoes by main force up the rapids, and since our water voyage ended, a no less desperate tussle through the dark, dense, tangled thickets, and by a track that seemed to lead us continually up-hill.

"As far as I can make out," proceeded the doctor, after a pause, " our guide has left the valleys that might be expected to bring us to the passes leading to the Salwen river, and is carrying us directly to the steepest parts of the dividing range, with what object I cannot imagine."

"Do you not think, sir," I asked, "that there has been something mysterious about Yung-wan's behaviour from the very beginning? You remember how reluctant he was to join us, and how eager he has been since to bring us into this quarter?"

"I would answer for his good faith with my life," said Tom hastily. "And well I might, for I owe mine to him and to Hannibal."

"I would too, sar," struck in the negro. "Dere is no harm in dat coloured man, Massa Doctah and Massa Bob. He quite right all frew."

"I do not doubt it," the doctor rejoined; "neither, I am sure, does Bob. What I have noticed is that he has some scheme in his head that he has not yet divulged to us. He seems in constant fear of being watched and surprised, though the hill-folks hereabout have been quite friendly. You observed in what a hurry he was to dismiss our canoemen, and the precautions he took, by doubling and returning on his path, to discover if they were following us. To-day he has been more excited and suspicious than ever, especially since we heard the rumour in the village where we made our mid-day halt that the rebel army in Yunnan had been scattered, and that some of the refugees were supposed to have fled for shelter to these mountains. And now, after his hard day's march, he has climbed up to the brow of the hill above to reconnoitre the position, and see if there are no spies about."

"Have you not asked him, then, sir, what he has in his head?"

"I have, but got no satisfactory reply. He insists that this is the only route. The fact is," proceeded the doctor, after a few moments' thought, "I have not been anxious to turn away from the line we are now following. I believe we are on the eve of the greatest discovery our journey has yet yielded. Look at these heights."

We turned towards the quarter indicated by our leader—the only direction in which we could see beyond the limits of the little glade where the guide had left us. We were now high above the level of the plains, and had left behind us the tropical jungle, but coppices of oak, birch, and bracken, growing amid rocks stained

white with lichens, shut out the landscape on three sides
of us. On the remaining side there opened up a prospect of dark valleys and of wooded hills rising to meet
a lofty range of mountains, whose peaks, standing out
grandly to the south-westward, reared themselves in
columnar masses, grouped together like the tubes of some
stupendous organ, or showed like vast lines of broken
wall capped by fragments of towers and overlooked by
domes and truncated cones, tilted this way and that, as
if the whole were in the act of tumbling into ruin. So
strange and wild was their appearance, that we had difficulty in persuading ourselves that we were not looking
upon a fantastically-shaped cloud that had formed itself
in the evening sky.. A cold wind blew from these unscalable heights, which were flecked with snow, and we
had already had a warning of the harsh climate of the
mountains in a shower of sleet. The doctor explained
to us that these rocks bore on their slopes the traces of
what he called " igneous action." They had been thrown
up, perhaps from the bottom of the ocean, when the
earth was heaving and bubbling with intense heat, and
it was possible that the fires that had formed them were
not yet extinct. We had seen many signs of recent
volcanic action, having crossed several brooks of warm
or tepid water close by ice-cold streams, and having this
very evening found a sulphur spring, so hot that we
could not bear to keep our hands in it.

"I should not wonder," said Dr. Roland in conclusion, "if we came upon a real, live, smoking volcano. It has often been conjectured that an active volcanic region would be found hereabout. It will be a feather in our caps if it has been reserved for us to discover it."

He was interrupted by Yung-wan, who appeared scrambling down the face of the rocks with the activity of a cat. The results of his survey had evidently pleased him; for, along with the suppressed excitement in his face, there was an air of triumph in the way he signalled to us to begin the ascent at once, as soon as he was fairly in view. He had satisfied himself apparently that there were no spies about; for instead of creeping cautiously up under cover, as on his first ascent, his only anxiety was now to get rapidly to the top. We followed him, wondering what was about to happen next, and hardly able to keep the guide in sight, so steep and rugged was the way. After half an hour's tough work we crested the ridge, and could see not only what lay beyond, but the whole country around us. As the doctor had already guessed, we were on the summit of one of the highest of the spurs thrown off from the dividing range between the Mekong and Salwen rivers. Looking behind us, we saw the ridge on which we were standing and a number of parallel ridges stretching away eastward, with steep valleys between, towards low, hot lands by the river. In front and on both sides of us was the majestic central chain, of which we had now a fuller view; and almost at our feet was a deep, desolate gorge that appeared effectually to bar our way. Beyond this gorge, and far away among other peaks, at a distance of probably thirty miles, was an object that instantly riveted our notice—a cone with a light blue vapour rising from its summit—a veritable volcano!

Yung-wan looked on impatiently, while the doctor noted as carefully as possible the position of the smoking crater, and we spoke excitedly about our discovery. He even muttered a word or two to the effect that the " fire nât " would be angry at his home being looked at, and might do us an injury. He wished to call our attention to something much nearer at hand—the mountain, in fact, of which the ridge we were standing upon formed a part. It was a huge mass of naked brown rock, rising some three thousand feet above us, and therefore probably nine thousand feet above sea-level. Its base must have been many miles in circuit, and its summit had that appearance of a long ruined wall that we observed in other giants of the range. It looked, in fact, as if the top had been blown off by some terrific explosion, which had strewn the fragments of the mountain over all the neighbouring slopes.

"And I have no doubt that is exactly what has happened," said the doctor, to whom I ventured to impart this notion. "Some time or other there must have been a fearful outburst of smoke and flame up there, and the air would be filled with fiery ashes and sulphurous fumes."

"It must have been warm times up here then," said Tom. "It would have been worth while seeing the flames belching up hundreds of feet into the air, and red-hot rocks raining down into the gorge there."

"Hardly worth the risk, Tom," said the doctor. "We will find it quite quiet now, I fancy—only an extinct crater, with perhaps some water at the bottom. I cannot imagine what in the world Yung-wan wishes with us up there, but I am glad we are to have the chance of seeing down the vent.—Time to turn in, boys," he added, looking at the clouds and at his watch.

Of course it would have been out of the question to have begun the ascent that evening, so we kindled a fire and made ourselves as snug as we could for the night under the shelter of some gnarled and stunted trees. To tell the truth, our quarters were not very comfortable. Rain and sleet began by-and-by to fall, and the wind rose, and moaned and howled and sobbed among the crags and hollows of the mountain. We were barely able to keep the fire of green wood alive in the wind and wet, and it gave out much more smoke than heat. The cold, raw air pierced to our bones; and as we sat shivering on the sodden ground and huddling together for warmth, we cordially agreed that we would gladly exchange our

present chilly camping-place for one in the swamps below, even with the mosquitoes for company. Our only
consolation was, that away on one spot of the murky
horizon we saw a yellowish glare, which must come from
the volcano—"our volcano," as we already began to
call it.

Daylight at length broke, and we rose and stretched
our cramped limbs, to which our thin damp clothes still
clung. Breakfast did not occupy us long, for Hannibal
had nothing better to offer than the cold remnants of a
bustard, knocked over on our yesterday's march and partly
devoured at last night's supper. The mountain did not
look any more inviting in the gray morning light; and
I never felt less inclined or able to devote myself to the
cause of science than on this occasion. Hannibal glanced
nervously at the smoking cone in the distance, above which
a dark cloudy shape now hovered, like one of the "gins"
of the Arabian Nights. Though as bold as a lion when
man or beast was in question, he was not above superstitious fears. The events of the night had shaken him,
and Yung-wan had tried to beguile the time by telling in
his broken English some horrifying tales of the baleful
power of the nâts of the mountains, and of the "beloos"
or demons of the wood—monsters with iron teeth and
nails, and eyes like live coals.

"Dere's nuffing to fear, Massa Tom," he said to Wilson,
whom he had taken under his special protection since

the adventure at the falls. Tom's teeth were chattering with cold, and Hannibal, whose own voice was quaking, thought it his duty to inspire his youthful companion with courage. "If one of dem ghosts come for us, he'll have to go away pretty quick. Massa Doctah is not de man to put up with nonsense from dese sort of folks, I tell you."

"Oh bother!" said Tom peevishly. "Do you think I am shaking for fear, like yourself, Han? I declare if these stories of Yung-wan's have not made your wool stick on end. Why, man, it must have been some tiger glaring at him from a thicket that he took for that preposterous 'beloo' of his, and his nâts were nothing more or less than vapour, like that above the burning mountain there. There's nothing to fear, Master Hannibal," he concluded, giving the worthy black a resounding slap on the back.

Nevertheless the party were not in high spirits when they began to climb the mountain, the exception being the guide, who seemed to grow secretly more elated with every yard of progress we made. The reader has heard enough by this time of hill-climbing, and need not be troubled with an account of this weary part of our day's work. The sun blazed out; and to make up for being half-frozen over-night, we were now half-roasted. The slopes were steep and rugged, and it was not easy to find a way over the black and brown rocks, the heaps of

scoriæ and ashes, and the streams of cooled lava, marking
the track of some former overflow of superheated
materials from the burning pit in the bowels of the
mountain. Rough grass, ferns, and some other plants
grew in tufts, but hardly in sufficient quantity to help
us much in our ascent; and a fine volcanic dust found
its way into our eyes, nostrils, and mouths, and almost
suffocated us. The sun had passed the meridian when we
halted on the top, in what seemed a sterile, blasted plain
strewn with ashes, cinders, and masses of black, fused
rock, like refuse from some vast furnace. In the centre
was a wide and deep depression, and approaching the
edge cautiously we peeped over into the abyss. It was
a great pit, of oblong shape, perhaps a mile in length
by a quarter of a mile in width, and surrounded by
nearly precipitous rocks, except on the side opposite to
us, where there was a gap in the walls of the crater.
Once this void had belched up smoke and flame and red-
hot ashes, and the mountain had trembled with the
shocks and echoed with the din of the terrible struggle
within it; but the silence of death and utter desolation
was now on the scene, and the gray gleam of water
five hundred feet below us showed that a lake occupied
the bottom of the vent.

We worked our way with much difficulty round to
the gap I have spoken of, and after a perilous descent
we stood on the margin of the lonely tarn. A stream

of water of a yellowish-red colour escaped from it, and flowed through the cleft and down a gloomy ravine beyond. We were now on the western side of the mountain, and the guide confirmed by a nod the doctor's opinion that this water must help to swell the flood of the Salwen. So dark and sinister was the scene, the black and blasted crags hemmed us in so closely and frowned on us so threateningly, that I could not help a feeling of mysterious awe and almost terror stealing over me, or wonder at the superstitious natives believing that this was a place where the evil spirits had peculiar power. We seemed utterly cut off from every other living thing, in a spot which had more of the features of the nether world than of the fair and sunshiny earth. The dark lake before us looked as if it were never visited even by the winds of heaven, though there was a kind of troubled movement on its surface—probably indicating the position of the springs—that made my flesh creep. About three hundred yards from us, and close under one of the cliffs, was a little island—a pinnacle of bare rock rising a few feet above the surface. The water must have been of profound depth, for on flinging in a stone quite close to the margin, we noticed the bubbles rising at the spot for nearly a minute.

As we were thus engaged we heard a splash close by us, and found to our surprise that Yúng-wan had divested himself of his clothes, had plunged into the lake, and was already swimming towards the island. Breathless with wonder and suspense, we watched him as he made his way to the rock. He did not remain there long, turning almost at once to regain the shore. It was not till he was within a few yards of us that we observed that he was in a state of extreme distress. With much trouble we succeeded in hauling him on shore, where he immediately sank down exhausted. He held out his right hand, which had been tightly clenched, towards the doctor, and opening it, disclosed a bluish-coloured pebble, in the form of a rough crystal. More puzzled than ever, Dr. Roland took it from him and examined it, while we no less narrowly scanned our chief's face. We saw breaking into it some of the excitement which we had noticed for some days past in our guide. He uttered an exclamation, and Yung-wan, forgetting his prostration, started to his feet.

"Why," cried the doctor at length, "this is a sapphire, and, I should think, one of the very finest and largest in existence! It must weigh five hundred carats at least. The man who possesses this is a prince."

He handed us the gem to look at. It was larger than a pigeon's egg—a crystal of six sides, terminating at each end in a six-sided pyramid. A pale blue shone through the roughened outer surface; but there was a chip on one of the sides, disclosing a lovely cerulean tint, matching one of the softest and deepest shades of the evening sky, and with a brilliancy of its own.   It was a gem of the "first water," only inferior to the diamond itself in value; and one could not look at it without the heart beating with pleasure in its extreme radiancy and beauty.

Dr. Roland handed the brilliant back to its owner; but Yung-wan refused it, signifying that he meant it as his offering of gratitude to his benefactor—the fee for having had his life preserved.   This, of course, the doctor would not hear of; and the guide was compelled reluctantly to take the gem back again into his keeping. He was now, if possible, more anxious to leave the lake than he had been to reach it; and sharing in his eagerness to escape from this forbidding place, we hastened down the bank of the stream, and entered the defile, amid the gathering shadows.

CHAPTER XIX.

LOST.

FOR some time we hastened on, hardly drawing breath to exchange a word with each other, as we slid or climbed over the blocks of lava and basalt with which the bed of the stream was paved. You would have said, had you seen us, that we were fleeing in panic, with all the host of evil genii of the mountains at our heels. And, in truth, we did feel like those heroes of the old romances, when they had borne away some potent ring or charm from an enchanted castle, and knew that the incensed magician was busy summoning his familiar spirits and working his wicked spells in order to bring down trouble and disaster upon them. It seemed as if a secret danger were brewing for us up by that "uncanny"-looking lake, and that our safety lay in getting quickly away from its lonely and desolate shores. There were more substantial reasons for pushing on, however. We had no desire to pass another night high up the mountain; and hunger was making impor-

tunate calls upon us, which we had no hope of satisfying
in that cold, deserted region behind us.

We had at last to come to a halt; for not only were
we exhausted by fasting and severe exertion, but the
darkness was gathering in so deeply that we could no
longer pick our way. We were fortunate enough to find
some nuts and berries on the shrubs that again began to
line our path,—and still better, a cool, fresh spring of
water; for we did not dare to drink the sulphury-
looking fluid by our side that ran down from the lake.
The pool also yielded a few "fresh-water oysters;" so
that our meal, though not enough to appease our
ravenous appetite, was perhaps better than we had any
right to count upon.

We had now time to hear the guide's story of the
finding of the great sapphire, and Yung-wan, after
carefully reconnoitring the ground to see that there
were no listeners near, had no hesitation in satisfying
our curiosity, as far as his limited power of expression
in English and Chinese went. He told us that he
belonged to this part of the country, or rather to the
district on the eastern side of the mountain we had just
crossed. He had been engaged at the famous ruby and
sapphire mines of the King of Burmah, which lay some
distance to the westward of where we now were; but
finding that any treasure he found was immediately
seized upon by the myrmidons of His Golden-footed

Majesty, the "Proprietor of the Mines of Rubies, Gold, and Silver," as he proudly styles himself, he left these profitless diggings in disgust, and made his way towards his home. Passing through the jungles near the mouth of the stream we were now following—which he told us fell into the Salwen little more than a day's journey ahead—he fell upon a spot which his experience of gem-workings told him was a likely place to find precious stones. He set to work to sift the gravel and sand with such tools as he could lay hands on, and ere long he came upon several small rubies and topazes. Thus encouraged, he went on secretly digging for several days, until he was rewarded by turning up the magnificent gem which we had seen.

His first feeling was one of stupefaction, then extreme elation, but lastly fear. How should he dispose of this treasure, which might make him the greatest and wealthiest man of his tribe, but was more likely to bring him trouble, or perhaps death? He dared not return to Burmah. The English he did not at that time know; and, besides, the country of the Red Karens, the sworn and deadly enemies of his race, lay between them and him. On the other hand, Chinese traders were in the habit of passing through his native country, and he knew them to be great dealers in jewels and stones of price. He resolved to make his way into China, and there find a merchant for the great sapphire.

But here also there were dangers to be encountered. The frontiers were in the hands of lawless bands of robbers, and there were rumours of insurrection having again broken out. A single unarmed man like himself would be certain to be plundered, and probably murdered. He must hide his gem, and bring a merchant to it who should have strength enough at his back to carry it off in safety. Then he bethought him of the lake in the crater. There could be no safer hiding-place; for apart from its secluded position, none of the natives of the district would venture near the spot, out of terror for the supernatural beings that were supposed to lurk there. In fear and trembling he ascended to the haunted tarn, and hid the sapphire in a cleft of the rocky islet in the centre. Then he made his way to China, which he reached almost naked, having been stripped by brigands of the lesser gems he had brought away with him, and barely escaping with his life. At the city of Yunnan-fu he had found a merchant whom he had convinced of the truth of his story. The scheme finally concocted was that a trading-party should be organized, and should start, as if proceeding by the usual direct trade route to Mandalay, with Yung-wan as guide. When they had reached the neighbourhood of these mountains, the Shan would lead them to the place where the sapphire was concealed; and it was hoped that through his influence, and by the aid of bribes, his tribe would be

engaged to form a strong convoy in carrying the gem
to China. In the party, as it turned out, was one of
the conspirators who were secretly engaged in stirring
up the Mohammedans to revolt, and this man, Yung-wan
suspected, had got an inkling of the true object of the
journey, and had betrayed them into the hands of his
ferocious leader, Khodja Akbar Khan. Had he not escaped, their intention, he believed, had been to spare his
life, and to induce him by torture, threats, and promises
to reveal the hiding-place of the sapphire. In Yung-wan's
opinion, the spies had never once taken their eyes off
him; and one of the first faces he noticed among the
party who surprised us at the ferry on the Mekong,
was that of his traitorous companion. Since our approach to the hiding-place of his treasure, and especially
after hearing the report that stragglers from the broken
rebel bands had been seen in the neighbourhood, his
suspicions of spies dogging his steps had redoubled.
Again on his knees, and almost with tears, he besought
the doctor to take the sapphire. He had not, he vowed,
once slept soundly or had a moment's ease of body or of
mind since the hour when its fatal beauty first gleamed
upon him like a star in the dark bosom of mother
earth.

Dr. Roland gently explained to him that it was out
of the question to accept such a gift at his hands.
"Besides," he added, with a smile, "if it has been such

a burden on you, my friend, it is hardly an act of kindness to wish to roll it over upon me. But I will tell
you what we will do. If you choose to guide us
thither, we will go with you to the spot where you
unearthed the sapphire. Who knows," he added, turning to us, "but we may each come away laden with
gems, as if we had come out of Aladdin's cavern."

To this the guide joyfully assented, telling us that
the place was only a few hours' march from our direct
route to the British border. Then we resigned ourselves to sleep, after arranging to keep a strict watch
in turns during the night. Nothing happened to disturb
us, except that towards morning Hannibal roused us,
and declared with great earnestness that he had seen a
dusky shape watching us, and that it immediately. disappeared from sight.

"Saw um flop right down b'hind dat dar bush, sar,"
he insisted, wiping the cold sweat from his brow, with
his eyes rolling in his head; but he could give no other
account of the apparition, except that it was as "big as
a bull" and had eyes "like live coals."

Tom thought we ought to "blaze away a bit" at the
shrub before approaching it, and I was inwardly of the
same opinion, but the doctor pointed, as one excellent
reason against "blazing away," that we had just one
rifle cartridge left. He stepped quietly up to the bush,
followed by the rest of us, when we found that though

it loomed so big in the foggy light, it could not have given cover to a catamount. We had a hearty laugh at Hannibal, which was none the less loud because he infected some of us with his half-superstitious fears, and scathing were the sarcasms as to how his "bull" had found shelter behind a few twigs of willow.

When day had fully broken, however, and our march was resumed, we found that we had not wholly shaken off the feeling of disquiet that had crept upon us from the moment that the sapphire had come into our charge. The scenery of the ravine through which we were wending was weird and oppressive in the extreme. The black, gaunt walls looked as if they had been scathed with fire, and plant and animal life seemed to be timorously venturing back into the valley after some terrible catastrophe that had laid it waste. We met with hot, bubbling sulphur springs; little water-courses that trickled down the rocks—the waters tinged with white, green, purple stains, and exhaling powerful gases; and basins from which puffs of steam and jets of water rose at regular intervals.

Yung-wan now told us, in an awe-stricken whisper, something that added not a little to our sense of alarm. On his last visit here, these snorting demons, as he firmly believed them to be, had not been nearly so active and violent. The stream that escaped from the crater and ran down the gorge was then a mere

dribblet; now it ran in a powerful current, that rose
above mid-leg when we forded it, and we even fancied
that it was stronger both in smell and in force since
yesternight.   But the most remarkable thing was what
he told us about the crater-lake.   When he had dipped
into it on the occasion when he had concealed the
sapphire, the water had a pleasant, hardly sensible
warmth.   On swimming to the island on this last visit,
he had crossed spots where water was welling up so
hot that he could scarcely bear it, and it was this that
had relaxed his powers and weakened his strength so
much that he was barely able to struggle back to the
margin.   Even at the edge we had found the tempera-
ture to be somewhat more than tepid.   We remembered
with dismay the signs of greater activity we had
noticed in the burning cone to the southward; and
from some words that the doctor let fall, we gathered
that an explosion of the volcano might occur at any
moment, though, on the other hand, it might linger on,
" getting up steam," for a month.

Was it the glamour of the great sapphire that made
us start and listen at every little sound we heard in
the jungle—the snapping of a twig, the rustling of a
branch, or the fall of a handful of earth from the rocks ?
We were more nervous and fearful in this forsaken dell
than we had been when surrounded by savages or
by bandits, or when plunging down the rapids of the

Vivian Drew.

X'mas, 1898.

Mekong. We "felt" danger rather than saw it, like men who, in the darkness, know that some malign thing is watching them, without being able to tell what or where it is. And yet, apart from the faint noises I have mentioned, and which may probably have been caused by some deer, or monkey, or bird, absolutely nothing disturbed the profound and deathly solitude.

The gorge widened a little as we advanced, leaving room for stunted trees on both banks, but the precipitous walls continued as high as before. Our midday rest was taken at a spot where the jungle began to be more tall and dense. We were talking over our plans in a less elated tone than might have been expected from people who had just "come into a fortune" —which, perhaps, might be explained by the fact that we had had nothing to eat since the morning—when the call of a bush-turkey was heard in the thicket not far off, and it fell musically on the ear of hungry men. Yung-wan, who was skilful in stalking this sort of game, stole into the jungle, armed only with a stick, and of course having his long knife stuck into his belt in case of coming suddenly upon a tiger or a panther, while we kept perfectly still in our places. After a pause the call was repeated a little further off; and then another interval of silence was startlingly broken by a loud shriek for help. We sprang to our feet. We heard sounds of scuffling, trampling, and breaking of branches,

(690) 16

as if a terrible struggle were going on, and we dashed through the thick undergrowth of thorns, the creepers, and the air roots, in the direction of the noise. All was quiet again when we reached the spot, except that we could hear the sound of retreating footsteps already some distance off. But our thoughts were soon wholly absorbed in an object on the ground. It was the body of the guide, motionless and covered with blood. The doctor bent over him, examined the wounds on his back and chest, and felt his pulse. Then he looked at us with an expression of face we understood too well. Yung-wan was dead! He had evidently been surprised from behind, and a mortal wound had been inflicted on him before he could defend himself; but he had had time before being overpowered to draw his knife, which he still held firmly clenched in his hand. He had not fallen alone, for a few paces off we found another bloody and lifeless form extended on the damp earth and leaves. It was that of a swarthy man, of the Chinese type of features, but wearing the white turban and other tokens of having belonged to the army of rebel Panthays. The doctor and Hannibal thought they had noticed his face in the group that surrounded the insurgent leader on the occasion of our capture; but Tom and I had to admit that the countenances of these people were so much alike that we could scarcely distinguish one from another.

We had no doubt, however, that this was the man about whom poor Yung-wan had told us, who had joined him in his first expedition and afterwards turned traitor; and we had not much difficulty in guessing who was the accomplice who had escaped.

On searching, we found that Yung-wan's girdle, in which, as we knew, the sapphire had been concealed, had been rudely torn open. The gem was gone! The knowledge also of the mine of precious stones, from which we had promised ourselves such untold wealth, had perished with its discoverer; for who could now guide us to the secret spot where he had found this fatal treasure? Little, however, did such reflections trouble us at first. We thought of the faithful, devoted fellow who had been our companion through so many dangers and hardships—of his unfailing courage and patience, his touching gratitude, and of the deep debt of thanks that we owed him in return. It was with sad and full hearts that we bore him to a cavity in the rocks, in lieu of a better sepulture. Beside him we laid the corpse of his assassin, and we rolled a large stone over the hole as a defence against the vultures.

CHAPTER XX.

FOUND.

WHEN the mournful duty was over, other ideas took possession of our minds. Anger succeeded to sorrow. We were filled with hot and fierce indignation against the cowardly villain who had so treacherously murdered our cheerful and kindly little guide, and we determined to track him down. It was scarcely possible that he could have doubled back without our seeing him; and besides, his obvious way of escape was down-stream. So we resumed our route with fresh vigour, keeping a sharp look-out to right and left for the fugitive. It seemed at first as if he had eluded us; but on reaching a more open part of the defile we came upon signs that showed us that we were in the right track, and gave us hopes that in spite of his start we would soon come up with the assassin. Drops of blood stained the stones—a proof that the man we were pursuing had not come scathless out of the struggle It was singular, and we could not

help remarking upon it even as we hurried on, that our
journey in unexplored lands should be ending as it had
begun, in a life-and-death chase through a rocky ravine.
But how different were the circumstances! Then we
were fugitives, fleeing for our lives before a band of
naked savages; now we were messengers of vengeance,
following hard on the steps of our wounded enemy.

By-and-by we came in sight of him labouring painfully along over the boulders and through the brushwood in front. As we rapidly gained upon him, he
cast a glance at us over his shoulder like the glare of a
hunted tiger. It scarcely surprised us to recognize the
face of Khodja Akbar; and he appeared to know that
the fates had pronounced against him, for his dark
features were convulsed with impotent fury and hate.
At this part of the valley there was a spot where it
was just possible to climb up the crags to the level
above; and his eye seemed to measure the distance
between us and him, in order to judge whether he had
time to avail himself of this loophole of escape. He
must have decided that he had not, for without pausing
he continued his flight down the valley.

We must now, according to what we had learned
from poor Yung-wan, be quite close to the Salwen,
which here, as throughout its course, flows in a confined
and narrow channel. Before entering the main river,
however, the small stream we had been following cast

itself over a steep cliff in a turbid waterfall.   Above the
fall the crags hung higher and grimmer than ever; while
aloft, fine forest trees, including the magnificent teak:
for which this region is so famous, spread out their
branches almost over the cascade.   Khodja Akbar, with a
lead now of little more than a hundred yards, crept along
the sides of the cliffs, until he reached a yawning gap,
close to the falling water, and crossed by a single tree-
trunk, which had to all appearance fallen accidentally
into this position from the forest above.   He stepped
across with wavering steps, and then seizing the end of
the log, he strained all his force to hurl it from the
rock.   At this moment, and several times before, the
doctor might, of course, have shot him dead; but he
shrank from taking the life of a fellow-creature, even
one caught red-handed, in this way, and to expend
our last cartridge on the deed.   The heavy trunk
would not be moved, and the fugitive turned again
for flight.   We had approached within a few yards
of this natural bridge, when I felt the solid ground
tremble, and then heave like the deck of a ship
at sea.   Thinking that a portion of the rock was
about to give way, I instinctively clung to the bushes
near me.   There was a brief pause, and then a violent
shock, two or three times repeated, and to my confused
senses the crags about me seemed to rock and reel;
large fragments detached themselves from the cliffs and

fell crashing to the bottom, and a loud splash announced that a mass of ponderous size had fallen into the water beneath, while a dull muffled sound like distant thunder reached my ears.

All this may have occupied only a few moments, but it appeared to me that at least a couple of minutes had elapsed before I had collected my scattered wits, and looked about me, dazed and giddy as if just recovering from a stunning blow. The tragic events of the last few hours—the assassination, the burial of the victim, the pursuit of the murderer—had driven from our minds all recollection of the danger that threatened us from the awakening volcano behind us, and this earthquake shock bewildered us at first by its unexpectedness. Almost the first thing I observed clearly was that an impassable chasm now barred our advance—the tree that crossed the chasm had been shaken from its place and was floating in the pool beneath. A mocking laugh from Akbar the Kashgaree, as he passed from sight round a projecting crag, told us that he also perceived that pursuit in this direction was hopeless.

There was nothing for it but to " hark back " to the spot where, as I have before mentioned, the cliffs seemed scalable. With infinite trouble the whole party succeeded at last in reaching the summit of the rocks. We found ourselves amid dense and lofty forests that almost covered the country in front as far as our view

extended, heaving and sinking, according to the irregu-
larities of the surface, like a vast sea of green.   The
teak tree, with its stately trunk and great pendulous
leaves, that have so often been compared to the ears of
an elephant, predominated; but there were also many
varieties of palms and other plants of the tropics, beautiful for their flowers or their foliage, or valuable for
the fruits, dyes, gums, drugs, and spices that they yield.
Within easy reach we descried the valley of the Salwen
lying like a deep trench across our way, just as we had
seen it in Thibet three or four hundred miles higher up,
when we had been slung across its restless waters on a
slim rope.   Its banks now, instead of being naked and
gaunt, were clothed with dense verdure; but they looked
scarcely less savage.   We knew, however, that when we
had reached the farther shore we should have left the
limits of the absolutely unknown behind us, and that
a few comparatively easy stages more would bring us
among our fellow-countrymen, for whose homely faces
and voices and home-like ways we were longing with
an energy that only those who have sojourned like us
in far and savage countries can understand.

We followed as closely as we dared the edge of the
cliffs, occasionally peering over to see if any traces of
Akbar were to be detected in the gorge below.   Unexpectedly we came in sight of him, resting on a rock not
far beneath the waterfall.   The pain of his wound had

overcome him, or he had met with some obstacle in front which he could not pass ; or perhaps he imagined that he was now safe from farther pursuit. We could almost have dropped a pebble upon the spot where he sat; but he had evidently no suspicion that we were so near to him.

As we leaned over the cliffs, discussing in low earnest tones what means we should take to bring our enemy to bay, a noise which we had heard for some minutes, and taken for the distant roar of a waterfall, smote more loudly on our ears. Every moment the volume of sound increased, and it seemed to be approaching us rapidly, and from the direction of the upper end of the valley. As we listened, it swelled into angry, terrible notes, that filled the air with foreboding and alarm. We looked at one another, already half conjecturing the truth before the doctor told us, by sign rather than by word, that the earthquake must have rent wider the gap in the mountain above, and that this must be the escaping waters of the lake in the crater that were hurrying towards us down the gorge. Khodja Akbar also had heard the sound, and had started to his feet. The fierce feeling of anger and desire for vengeance which had inspired us during the last few hours seemed to pass away when we saw the poor, wounded wretch exposed to so appalling a doom. There was one particular part of the cliffs where, with our help from above,

it was just possible for him to reach a place of safety.
We shouted to him at the highest pitch of our voices, and
eagerly signalled to him where he should go.   He turned
towards us, but he could not or would not understand
our meaning.   Perhaps it was already too late, for the
flooded stream was already thundering down the rocky
channel in ponderous brown masses.   The doomed man
shrieked some words—a prayer or an imprecation—
which were lost in the noise of the torrent.   He shook
his fist at us, and something gleamed an instant in his
hand.   Was it the knife with which he had slain his
brother man; or was it the great sapphire, for the sake
of which he had steeped his hand in innocent blood?
I cannot tell; for at that instant the main body of the
flood reared itself above the rocks at the fall, like a
chafed and angry lion, with a tawny mane of rushing
waters streaming behind it.   Another moment, and it
had leaped down with a mighty roar on its solitary
victim, and the body of Akbar was tumbling and tossing amidst the wreck of uprooted trees and broken
reeds that were hurrying down to the " Valley of the
Shadow."

There is not much of the story of our journey left for
me to tell.   We turned away horror-stricken from the
scene we had witnessed; yet soon there came a feeling
of intense relief, for the constant strain of suspense and

suspicion that had weighed upon us so long as we were under the shadow of the volcanoes, with the great sapphire in our charge, and an unsleeping enemy near us, was now removed.   We reached the huts of a party of teak-cutters and rafters, kindly people that entertained us hospitably while we rested to recruit and to prepare for resuming our journey. Some attempts we made convinced us that it was hopeless to expect to discover poor Yung-wan's sapphire-mine.   After waiting until the flood had abated, we proceeded down the swift Salwen for several days on one of the timber-rafts that descend to the sea even from this distance up the river. We had plenty of dangerous experiences in shooting rapids and slipping past rocks, but nothing that we were not by this time well inured to.   Then came vexing delays; for there were alarming rumours that a hostile tribe had formed a stockade on the river, and the raftsmen would not proceed until they were certain that the way was clear. We determined to leave the stream, and, hiring a party of guides and porters, proceed over-land to the border of British Burmah, now close at hand.

On the third morning we were marching through a jungly forest of " toddy palms" and bamboos, when the alarm was given from the front that there was a tiger in the path. Sure enough we found a great yellow brute growling and snarling, on the opposite bank of a marshy stream, over the body of a deer which he had brought down, and was loath to leave. Dr. Roland was about to fire—we had replenished our stock of ammunition from our friends on the river—when the sharp crack of a rifle resounded in the wood, and the tiger rolled over, clawing and tearing up the ground with his huge paws.

"You've done it this time, Sandy," said a hearty voice in the beloved tongue of our native England. "Right through the ear, too, as I am a living man."

"I think the shot might have been worse," said another voice in slower and more deliberate tones, in which might easily be detected the accents of one born to the north of the Tweed. "But what could the beast mean by glowering across the burn in yon way?"

Two stalwart figures, clad in half-military, half-sportsman dress, with white "puggerees" and leggings, came up to the spot where the tiger lay. Our surprise was nothing to theirs when we hailed them in their own language. And truly strange tatterdemalion figures we must have seemed as we emerged with our native followers from the brake, with our sunburned features, unkempt locks, and ragged jackets. Our new friends were Lieutenants Alexander M'Leod and Henry Verney, of the Royal Engineers. They had been sent out on the duty of marking off the frontier between the Karen tribes and the country claimed by independent Burmah, and having completed their task, had set off on a hunting trip

beyond the borders before returning to their station, when good fortune cast them in our path. I will not repeat what these kind officers said when they heard the story of our adventures. I know they made Tom and me blush till our faces tingled, with their praises of what they were pleased to call our gallantry and forti- tude, and shook our hands and slapped our backs with their heavy palms until it needed all our fortitude to prevent us from wincing. But we knew all the time— and told them so, only they would pay no heed to us— that we had really no credit for what had been done, having merely done our best to obey orders, and that to Dr. Roland, along with faithful Hannibal, the honour and glory of the journey really belonged.

That night we slept under canvas, in a clean ham- mock, after a warm and abundant meal, thus suddenly coming into the enjoyment of three comforts to which we had long been strangers. This was nothing, how- ever, to the delight of being again with friendly, hos- pitable people of our own nation, and of hearing news from home in our sweet mother tongue. We knew that our trials were over, and that we had got back again within the pale of civilized life, with the first glimpse we got of Lieutenant M'Leod's red whiskers and his companion's ruddy cheek.

A fortnight later we were in Rangoon, the capital and chief port of British Burmah. I need not narrate these later stages of our journey, which was through a country pretty well known already. The sights of Rangoon itself the reader will not thank me to describe, for it is a place visited by hundreds of British ships every year. To tell the truth, I have a very indifferent remembrance of them; for after our severe fatigue and privation, the whole party suffered from reaction, and for many days were hardly able to stir about. Our first duty, of course, was to send a message to Mr. Marshall and to our relatives at home, who, we found, had long given us up as lost. It was settled that we should not return to Assam, but proceed directly to England to recruit from the effects of our sojourn among the grim deserts of Thibet and the poisonous marshes of the Mekong.

One morning we stood on the deck of the steamer at the chief outlet of the Irrawady. We had bid good-bye to all our kind friends in Rangoon, and were about to set sail for " home." Tom and I were looking over the bulwarks watching the smooth current of the noble stream, covered with large and small craft, that we had crossed when it was little more than a mountain torrent, and the level green banks, with the roofs of pagodas, churches, and villas rising above the trees, so strangely in contrast to the wild and desolate scenes through which we had seen it flow near its source. Dr. Roland was close behind us, with Hannibal beside him, giving the finishing touches to the packing of his master's luggage. The doctor caught the last remark—something that Tom or I had said half-seriously and half-jocularly to the effect that, notwithstanding all the weary miles our feet had trodden, and the untold wealth we had had in our grasp, we were leaving these shores empty-handed.

"Empty-handed!" he echoed. "What do you call empty-handed? That case that Hannibal is strapping contains treasures worth—if the world only knew its real value—all the gold-mines in Burmah. There are specimens there that will make some of our men of science open their eyes."

"If we could have brought away the sapphire, wouldn't they have opened them wider still?" Tom slyly ventured to say.

"And even if you were empty-handed," the doctor proceeded, without paying attention to the interruption, "you are not empty-headed, or it is your own fault. Think on the rare and beautiful things that Nature has shown to you—the grand and mysterious secrets she has trusted you with, as the reward for visiting her in her solitude. Think of the knowledge of strange races and lands and customs you have learned, not through the medium of books or of teachers, but at first hand. Above all, boys, I think the trials and dangers we have come through together must have taught each one of us priceless lessons that we shall not forget to our dying day—lessons of faith and hope, of fortitude and manliness, of mutual forbearance and patience and helpfulness. Our pioneering in Further India has made us a few years older, but it has made us many years wiser."

Then the steam-whistle sounded, and our vessel got under way for England.

THE END.